OBiwumi

DON'T
BLAME
WOMEN

Yahweh Bless You

1Pet 5:10

BOOKS BY THE AUTHOR

The Prophetic Ordinance Blessing

Firstborn Syndrome

Don't Blame Women

Holy Spirit Manufactured Prayer – English

Gebet Vom Heiligen Geist Produziert
(Holy Spirit Manufactured Prayer – Deutsch)

Holy Spirit Manufactured Prayer – Spanish

Available at www.JesusintheHouse.org

Also at Xulon Press and
Bookstores Worldwide

RE-DISCOVERING
THE FIRST WOMAN IMPEACHED

DON'T
BLAME
WOMEN

She was NOT at the Naming Ceremony

MATTHEW DARE O'DUNLAMI

Don't Blame Women
She was NOT at the Naming Ceremony
Re-Discovering the First Woman Impeached
by Matthew Dare O'Dunlami

Printed in the United States of America

ISBN 9781629522289

Reference: Young's Analytical Concordance to the Bible by Robert Young; May 2011 and Strong's Exhaustive Concordance of the Bible by James Strong Updated July 2011.

Please take note that the name satan and other related names are not capitalized. This is intentional so as not to give him the honor of capitalizing his names, even to the point of violating grammatical rules.

Contact:
Matthew Dare O'Dunlami
Jesus in the House Ministries Inc. (JITH Ministries)
P. O. Box 567, Sicklerville, NJ 08081, USA
Email: Jithbooksministries@gmail.com
www.JesusintheHouse.org

www.xulonpress.com

DEDICATION

To the Alpha and Omega, Shepherd and Bishop of Souls, Lord Jesus Christ: Thank you for the revelation knowledge of your word inspired through me to accomplish this magnificent project for humanity.

To my late mother; Comfort Lola O'Dunlami, the first woman in my life, who I remembered vividly growing up, when about to sleep or whenever opportune to pray, she always sat next to my bed praying and groaning, for my future and destiny, until I fell asleep. In January 2003 she left this world to meet her Creator. But today, I can still hear my mother's voice whispering the word of God to my ear through her prayers.

Thank you again, Mom! The words you and Dad had spoken concerning me, from my birth to my adult life are true information and firmly rooted in the knowledge of God. These words shaped my destiny and inspired me to write this insightful and powerful book.

Thanks to my beloved wife, Esther, and my precious children, Comfort, Prince, Matthew, Patrice and Charles who continue to allow me to spend nights and days immersed in the pages of research for revelations of Christ and to produce this magnificent work of God. Thank you and I love you all.

To my sister, Evangelist Julianah Taiwo and her husband, Pastor Samuel Taiwo and my nephew, Dr. Joseph Taiwo for your support, I love you all.

To the entire human race, the descendants of Adam and Eve, I personally dedicate this book to men and women in His vineyard, around the globe and the seven continents. This book will find you joy, hope, peace, new revelation and understanding of true knowledge, of the word of God. Thank you for laboring in God's vineyard.

TABLE OF CONTENTS

PREFACE

This book *Don't Blame Women* is not about the first lady on the earth, but about the entire human race and how human behavior, characteristics, benefits, motivations, decisions, information and knowledge has imparts to us from creation, until the present. The benefits we seek, the decisions we make, the information we gather and the knowledge we aggressively acquire today, will determine our tomorrow. Does who you're talking to you really matter? Whose voice are you hearing behind you? Factors such as, benefits, motivations, decisions, information and knowledge, in their various forms, will shape the future and determine your effectiveness in this temporary orbit we call home.

Every decision you make or receive from someone, started with a particular motivation: the benefit you expect. Ask yourself, what is the motivating factor behind your decision? It's always inspiring to see the benefits of any of the decisions we have made. We always eagerly anticipate how each decision is unfolding. What could motivate you to make certain important decisions, knowing that such decisions could ultimately be detrimental to your lives and the people that surround you? Sometimes this decision might be vague or formless at the time you are making it, but you are still looking at the motivation, that is, the benefit behind it.

Don't Blame Women: She was not at the Naming Ceremony is quite different from any book I have written before. In 2012, the title was birthed in my spirit about 39,000 miles above the sea level while on an airplane to Europe, on a first-time, three-week crusade, in Germany. Suddenly, His voice came while I was trying to finish reading one of my books: *Holy Spirit Manufactured Prayer.* I had made the decision and desired in my heart that between the plane's take-off from the USA and landing in Frankfurt, Germany, that I would read this prayer book from the beginning to end. It was a conscious decision and the benefit and motivation was to fulfill one of the mandates of God; to pray without ceasing. In the middle of my long flight while reading, I heard His Voice clearly saying, "Matthew, **do not blame the woman.**" I replied, "Why?" and the Voice replied again to me, "She was not at the naming ceremony."

Many questions arose within me and inspiration by the Holy Spirit took over and began directing me through scriptures for further findings. Below, I asked the Holy Spirit many questions and He replied to the point of writing this book, based on the information shared with me, during my flight. As a result, I was able to minister from the material. It is true, when He said to us, He will tell you what to say at the hour.

These are the questions that came to mind:

1. Who was Lucifer before he became the serpent?
2. What did the serpent look like before he was cursed?
3. What language did Lucifer speak when he was cast out?

4. Did the serpent fly, walk, crawl or what body-form did he take?
5. What appearances has the serpent manifested lately?
6. What benefit is motivating your enemy?
7. What language did God use to speak to all of His creations?
8. What information does the enemy know about you?
9. Why was the woman made last, after all other living creatures?
10. Did Adam deliberately name his wife Eve after the deception?
11. What information are you volunteering to your enemy?
12. What type of decisions are you making?
13. Who is making decisions and suggestions for you?
14. Does whom I speak to or dialogue with matter?
15. Do you know that whatever you are hearing will determine your life?
16. What did God first tell His creations in the beginning?
17. What do you hear God saying to you?
18. What is motivating your decisions?
19. What information are you seeking?
20. Who are you seeking knowledge from?
21. Whose voice are you hearing?

In September 11, 2001 our country, the United States of America went through the biggest national catastrophe in its history, which caused many lives to be wasted. It did not just happen in 2001, but we are still reaping the harvest today, of what began in the Garden of Eden. Lucifer was motivated, because of the benefits he stood to gain by attacking God and humanity. The motivations and benefits of one person, residing in a remote cave area, induced and deceived his followers to attack a nation. The decision of one person can steal, kill and destroy so many. So, who is speaking to you?

Again, in 2008 the national economy of the United States collapsed significantly and caused many citizens to lose jobs, homes, health, insurance, families, relationships, lives and so forth. This has devastated the country and today is still affecting many around the nation. Others still haven't been able to recover from the impact of decisions made by the government and individual citizens. The economic decisions of one nation like the United States of America, has greatly impacted the world economy. Therefore, the outcome of economic decisions made by the United States has not only affected American citizens, yet the negative impact has spilled over to other nations. It is all about money, but because of false assumptions and greed, it has brought reproach and shame, even to the point of death to many.

One decision could result in death, and this happened to our first parents, in the Garden of Eden. After you knew well that you have the right thing in your mind, by His Spirit, why would you listen to a stranger's voice within and around you. Lucifer entered the serpent and became the stranger's voice to the first vulnerable woman on the earth. He enticed her, seduced her and caused her to make a dreadful decision.

Many people were involved with various mortgage financing schemes in the United States and bankers were more than willing to help them achieve the ultimate American dream. Because as we all know, the motivation for banks, is profit. Many people ran into error and took some of the equity on their house that already been paid off and pulled funds from their retirement saving accounts to buy a new home. 'Everyone is qualified', they said. Bank balance sheets got stronger and healthier while the mortgage financers were laughing all the way to the bank, each time a deal is closed. The surprise came when the real estate market crashed and people lost the greatest asset of their portfolios, which they had been building for many years. This was the result of bad decisions made by banks, finance companies and private citizens. The eyes of many were surely opened after they already fallen victim and realized their horrible mistakes.

Should these vulnerable citizens be blamed for their decisions? The first woman was deceived by the serpent, also were the citizens who got these seductive mortgages were deceived by the banker. Satan is the motivator and inducer of the first woman's decision, he was also the motivator for banks and inducer of the citizens' decisions. What benefit is motivating your decisions?

Incidentally, the LORD revealed to me five years before the mortgage market crash and that it will take seven years for a full economy recovery. I shared these messages in various churches about the upcoming event and eventual the fall of the mortgage market. Some people heard, believed, making the necessary adjustments and continue to benefit today. These people benefitted because it was a decision to listen to guidance coming from above and not from a man or stranger.

Don't Blame Women: She was not at naming ceremony, will help you find answers to the divine purpose in life; through benefits, decisions, information and knowledge, we acquire from our source, the Creator.

PROLOGUE

The role of women has been important in humanity since the beginning of creation, through to the present age. This book examines the revelation concerning the first woman, Eve, and the role she played in the fall of man and humanity's ongoing struggle with sin.

Our Creator desired from His heart to create woman, so then He made her to be great. God created the role, specifically for her most thus enabling her to participate in the task given Adam and the woman, fulfilling the mandate over God's creation. Therefore, the woman was qualified, inspired, motivated and encouraged of the things of God. She was positioned and entrusted by God over all things on the earth, above and below. The woman's dual responsibility on the earth is not to just have oversight, but to please both her husband and the Creator.

The woman's role is vital to the effectiveness of mankind and to all of humanity, which the LORD had planned and created. Eve was wandering and admiring the magnificent works of the Creator, in the Garden of Eden, when she ran into another creature of God, yet unfamiliar to her. During the cause of getting acquainted with the nature of the land, in which she has been placed, she met and engaged in an awful dialogue, with this unfamiliar new creature.

This unfamiliar creature, the serpent, had thought in his mind to present and share with the woman additional information besides what the Creator had previously told them when He placed them in the garden. Genetically, women are made to love and please everyone, especially their husbands.

This case was not quite different, so she entertained and trusted this unfamiliar creature, a stranger, with the information presented to her. The woman was created to please her husband and others, so she demonstrated her love by entertaining the stranger and sharing the new information she received from this unfamiliar being, with her husband. She was vulnerable.

The woman was vulnerable to all God's creatures, including the serpent. She trusted the serpent and received the information presented to her as valuable. God knew how important the woman's task would be for humanity, especially when He created a companion for Adam. If it were not so, the woman would have not been created. God created everything both male and female, because Adam alone could not achieve and accomplish the mandate God had set.

The purpose for which the woman was created is to help man achieve the following assignments and responsibilities that God desired and gave to humanity. He told them to be fruitful, multiply, fill the earth, subdue it and have dominion over all things in the sea, air and earth. It is a great responsibility and honor from God to put mankind; man and woman together in charge of all the wonderful things He has made.

The responsibility of the assignments between Adam and the woman were supposedly equally shared. Adam was privileged to certain information and was only made known to him and not to his wife. Creator brought all the animals to him to name them, one by one. He named them and also named the serpent. There is also certain information, which the woman should have been aware, but was only made known to man. This happened when Adam was inspired by God to name all the animals. Did Adam know the serpent's body form or type before it was cursed?

God made man first in His own image and then he made animals, and all the beasts of the field. He looked at man and desired from His heart that man could not accomplish the task ahead of him successfully, except He made him a woman. Among all God's creatures, God made the woman last. The woman became Adam's wife. The animals previously made could not possibly help Adam to achieve the task and responsibility God set ahead of him, for the sake of humanity, so He made him a woman.

There are degrees of information for everyone on the earth. The degree of information is vital and can only be measured by the result you derive from it. Falsely motivated information is detrimental to the existence of humanity. The information we receive into our hearts, comes from our desire for that knowledge. Today in our society, we are bombarded and brainwashed with all kinds of information. On several occasions, we have heard that, the more information you know, the better it is for you. That is true to a certain degree, but what kind of information are you getting and from whom are you getting this information. That is the reason why most people spend a significant amount of time and money on education. The mountain of information and knowledge one has, however, will seldom determine the journey of your life and those around you. What information do you have and where do you seek such information? Your journey in life will depend on your decisions made today and resulting actions to follow-up.

The false information officer, called the serpent and the stranger who appeared first at the beginning of creation and is still roaming around today. He is still roaming around giving different kinds of information to mankind, in order to exit believers from their role and purpose, for which they were created. When we look at today's society, we can see clearly that humans are driven by information. This desire for knowledge was initially imparted to mankind by Lucifer, the enemy of God. He had a different agenda and motivation; therefore he fabricated his own false information.

What information do you have? Who are you sharing your information with? Do you have false or true information? One person that can provide you true information, His name is called Truth. What information are you getting? Remember, the benefit you anticipate is the driven by the factor to seek and desire knowledge.

INTRODUCTION

By His knowledge the depths were broken up,
and clouds drop down the dew. (Proverbs 3:20)

Knowledge is a spirit and is also one of the seven Spirits of God, according to Isaiah 11:2. Those who seek His Spirit receive His anointing, wisdom, understanding, counsel, might, knowledge, and fear of Him. The tree of life was in the middle of the garden, and also the tree of the knowledge of good and evil was in the middle of the garden. Therefore God, the Alpha and Omega, prepared these two distinguished trees, life and death, in the middle of the garden. The tree of life bears the fruit of life, while the tree of the knowledge of good and evil bears the fruit of death. The tree of death was forbidden for them to eat or touch. The tree of death (good and evil) cannot be considered as the tree of death until the aspirants disobeyed the word that God had spoken to them. He gave both angels and mankind His free will, as well as the resulting consequences, to all decisions made.

The tree of the knowledge of good and evil was the only tree in the entire garden that God warned them not to eat or touch, or they will die. Firstly, when Adam and his wife were formed in the likeness of God, they were made pure and holy without darkness. This tree bears two different kinds of fruits: good and evil. However, have you ever seen a monkey that brought forth two different kinds of offspring, for example, a monkey and a gorilla? That is not natural. Have you ever seen a person that has reproductive organs of both male and female? This is abnormal. Also, have you ever seen a mango tree bearing both mangos and oranges? Can an apple tree bear both oranges and apples? That is not normal either. A mango tree only bears mangos, so also an orange tree only bears oranges. In this case, the tree of knowledge, in the middle of the garden, bears both the good and evil fruit on it. God warned Adam not to eat it or he will surely die.

> *And out of the ground the LORD God made every tree grow that is pleasant to the sight and good for food. The tree of life was also in the midst of the garden, and the tree of the knowledge of good and evil. (Genesis 2:9)*

> *But of the tree of the knowledge of good and evil you shall not eat, for in the day you eat it you shall surely die" (Genesis 2:17)*

The Lord had planned and provided all things for Himself and for humanity, before the creation of the world and made available to us what we will need, including our free will. He is the life, and the only One who can give life abundantly. Therefore, He placed the tree of life in the middle of the garden and did not tell them not to eat from it. God had already placed in Adam and Eve His Spirit of knowledge, when they were made because He breathed His Spirit into them. But Satan still found ways to deceive her.

> *And I have filled him with the Spirit of God, in wisdom, in understanding, in knowledge, and in all manner of workman-ship. (Exodus 31:3, 35:31)*

In the physical world, according to the nature of God, He created every tree to bear its own kind of fruit. The tree of the knowledge of good and evil that was forbidden to eat or touch in the garden, represents death for humanity, if they disobeyed Him. In the Scriptures, God told them "*...but of the tree of the knowledge of good and evil **you shall not eat,** for in the day that you eat of it you shall surely die.*" (Genesis 2:17) When Serpent, the deceiver asked the woman, Has God indeed said, "*You **shall not eat of every tree** of the garden?*" (Genesis 3:1) Yes indeed God told them not to eat, but on the other hand, the serpent didn't fully know what God had told them. Satan always hears in parts. He sniffs around to found out the full story about us, so that he may use it against us.

When God created Adam and his wife, they were pure and holy. There was no trace of darkness in them. God told Adam and his wife they should not eat and touch the forbidden fruit. That is the reason why Adam's wife was able to repeat fully what God had previously told them. Since satan and his agents never know the full story and always hear in parts; ask yourself what information you may have volunteered to him?

Always hold on to the word you have received or heard from God. Do not tell or share it with strangers! God spoke to Adam and his wife with the heavenly language (His Spirit), which Satan did not understand. God breathed on them and made them living beings. They were pure and holy because they were carrying the holiness and purity of God. Therefore, what came from the mouth of Adam's wife was what God had told them. The first woman was not contaminated until they obeyed Satan.

One example in which someone pursued wisdom and knowledge, but pleased God, is King Solomon. King Solomon asked from God when he knew he lacked the wisdom and knowledge to govern his people. He sought God, not other beings.

> *Now give me wisdom and knowledge, that I may go out and come before this people; for who can judge this great people of yours. (2 Chronicles 1:10)*

> *Then God said to Solomon: "Because this was in your heart, and you have not asked riches of wealth or honor or the life of your enemies, nor have you asked long life but have asked wisdom and knowledge for yourself, that you may judge My people over who I have made you king." (2 Chronicles 1:10-11)*

> *"Wisdom and knowledge are granted to you; and I will give you riches and wealth and honor, such as none of the kings have had who were*

before you, nor shall any after you have the like."
(2 Chronicles 1:12)

Pride and disobedience are enemies of our souls. The wisdom of God speaks better things to our spirit and heart, while knowledge addresses your body and soul. Scriptures illustrate that wisdom enters your heart, and knowledge is pleasant to your soul. Seeking God allows us to receive knowledge from Him directly.

> *For my people are foolish, they have not known Me; They are silly children, And they have no understanding: they are wise to do evil, But to do good they have no knowledge. (Jeremiah 4:22)*

> *Inasmuch as an excellent spirit, knowledge, understanding, interpreting dreams, solving riddles, and explaining enigmas were found in this Daniel, whom the King named Belteshazzar, now let Daniel be called, and he will give the interpretation. (Daniel 5:12)*

> *...that you may walk worthy of the Lord, fully pleasing Him, being fruitful in every good work and increasing in the knowledge of God; (Colossians 1:10)*

Since the garden, man has fallen progressively in the transgression of sin. As a result, humanity has been searching by all means and at all costs, for the tree of knowledge, in more ways than ever before. Most importantly though, the knowledge we need comes from Him.

> *My people are destroyed for lack of knowledge. Because you have rejected knowledge, I also will reject you from being priest for Me; Because you have forgotten the law of your God. I also will forget your children. (Hosea 4:6)*

Knowledge has become the center and core of living on earth. Ask yourself, which tree are you eating from? Are you eating from the tree of life through Jesus Christ? Or are you eating from the tree of death and from satan? Christ is the main tree and the true vine, which we ought to eat from. The knowledge that mankind is seeking today is not from God, but is from this dark world.

> *Grace and peace be multiplied to you in the knowledge of God and of Jesus our Lord. (2 Peter 1:2)*

> *For if, after they have escaped the pollutions of the world through the knowledge of the Lord and Savior Jesus Christ, they are again entangled in them and overcome, the latter end is worse for them than the beginning. (2 Peter 2:20)*

Knowledge is a spirit and is a Spirit of the Creator. (Isaiah 11:2) Those who will eat of it must know His Word. The word of God brings the revelation knowledge of Christ. While the free will benefit is still in place, think first. There is a choice we make in our lives, life or death. Remember, the determining factor of our life choices, depends entirely on the source of where one is seeking and gaining knowledge.

CHAPTER ONE

CREATIONS OF ANGELS

Let no one say when he is tempted, "I am tempted by God";
for God cannot be tempted by evil, nor does He Himself
tempt anyone. (James 1:13)

The All Sufficient God created heaven and earth and all that inhabit them. First, the Lord of Hosts created Angels to serve and worship Him. The names of some of the angels are mentioned in the Holy Bible. God used them greatly in the past and continues to use them today. The Creator of heaven and earth is holy. Therefore, there was no taint of maliciousness among any of the angels He created. Some of these angels are *Cherubim, Seraphim, Michael, Gabriel, Raphael, Uriel and Lucifer.* These angels were perfect and their primary purpose in heaven is to exalt their Creator. Some of these angels were assigned to perform certain responsibilities, for our ancestors on earth.

Angels are spirits and we have seen throughout Scripture how God mobilized them for specific assignments, as He commanded.

After God dragged man out of the Garden of Eden, because of their disobedience to His word, He assigned Cheribum, whom He placed at the east of the Garden of Eden, to guard and protect the tree of life. (Genesis 3:24)

Also note in scripture, that since the first day Daniel prayed, God answered him. But the prince of the kingdom of Persia withstood the angel of God from delivering his blessing until the angel Michael, one of the Chief Princes, came to help this angel. (Daniel 10:10-13) Also we have experienced the presence of the angel, Gabriel, significantly in the Scriptures. God had used him to deliver glad tidings to Zachariah, about his wife, Elizabeth, that she will have a baby called John the Baptist.

> *And the angel answered and said to him, I am Gabriel who stands in the presence of God, and was sent to speak to you and bring you these glad tidings. (Luke 1:19)*

LORD God also sent the angel Gabriel to Mary, to carry the Good News that she will have a Son called Jesus. (Luke1: 26). There are many angels that God used throughout scripture, and some have taken human form to deliver their messages from God to man.

Angels are spiritual, living-beings, who were also created to fulfill God's desires. They are messengers, overseers and deliverers of God's ordinances, whether for reward or punishment. When these angels interact with human beings, they can be invisible, audible, and can take on the human form, in order to accomplish whatever task God has commanded them. Sometimes, Jesus Christ the Son of God, is referred to as the

Angel of God, or the Angel of the Lord. Angels can be grouped into nine types, according to their tasks. They serve in various capacities, according to their hierarchy and rank. They are also grouped into three different spheres or choirs as God commanded them. The LORD God is the Creator of all angels.

First Sphere of the Angels of God

In the first sphere or specialty, the angels of God in heaven are separated into three distinguished and specialized groups, Seraphim, Cherubim and Thrones.

Seraphim: These angels are the closest to God. They praise God and represent His love. (Please note that Lucifer, before he became satan, was the highest of the Seraphim or anointed Cherubim). There are only four of them and their primary mission is to protect the throne of God. They have six wings: two cover their face; two on their body and two cover their feet.

> *Above it stood seraphim; each one had six wings: with two he covered his face, with two he covered his feet, and with two he flew. And one cried to another and said: Holy, holy, holy is the LORD of hosts: The whole earth if full of His glory (Isaiah 6:2-3)*

> *Then one of the Seraphim flew to me, having in his hand a live coal which he had taken with the tongs from the altar. And he touched my mouth with it, and said (Isaiah 6:6)*

Cherubim: These angels are the second highest of nine, in the hierarchy of angels. They are the intercessors of God. Their mission is also to protect the throne of God. They are fierce angels. When they come to earth, they are the great power of apocalypse nature. They have four faces: one of cherub, one of a man, one of a lion and one of an eagle. (*Exodus 25:18-20, Ezekiel 10:14-21*)

And you shall make two cherubim of gold; of hammered work you shall make them at the two ends of the mercy seat. Make one cherub at one end, and the other cherub at the other end; you shall make the cherubim at the two ends of it of one piece with the mercy seat. And the cherubim shall stretch out their wings above, covering the mercy seat with their wings, and they shall face one another; the faces of the cherubim shall be toward the mercy seat. (Exodus 25:18-20)

Each one had four faces: the first face was the face of a cherub, the second face the face of a man, the third the face of a lion, and the fourth the face of an eagle. And the cherubim were lifted up. This was the living creature I saw by the River Chebar. When the cherubim went, the wheels went beside them; and when the cherubim lifted their wings to mount up from the earth, the same wheels also did not turn from beside them. When the cherubim stood still, the wheels stood still, and when one[b] was lifted up,

32

the other lifted itself up, for the spirit of the living creature was in them. Then the glory of the Lord departed from the threshold of the temple and stood over the cherubim. And the cherubim lifted their wings and mounted up from the earth in my sight. When they went out, the wheels were beside them; and they stood at the door of the east gate of the Lord's house, and the glory of the God of Israel was above them. This is the living creature I saw under the God of Israel by the River Chebar, and I knew they were cherubim. Each one had four faces and each one four wings, and the likeness of the hands of a man was under their wings. (Ezekiel 10:14-21)

Thrones: Their name literally means thrones or ornamented chair. These angels dispense God's divine judgment. The lower hierarchies of angels need the thrones to gain access to God.

For by Him all things were created that are in heaven and that are on earth, visible and invisible, whether thrones or dominions or principalities or powers. All things were created through Him and for Him. (Colossians 1:16.)

Second Sphere of the Angels of God

The second sphere or specialty of the angels of God, are also separated into three distinguished and specialized groups: the Dominions, Virtues and Power.

Dominions: These are angels of leadership, regulating the duties of the angels. They give power to heads of government and other authority figures. They have the appearance of humans with wings.

> *For by Him all things were created that are in heaven and that are on earth, visible and invisible, whether thrones or dominions or principalities or powers. All things were created through Him and for Him. (Colossians 1:16)*

Virtues: These angels are known as the spirits of motion and control the elements. They govern all nature and perform miracles. They provide courage, grace, and boldness.

> *Who has gone into heaven and is at the right hand of God, angels and authorities and powers having been made subject to Him. (1Peter 3:22)*

Power: These angels have the task of controlling the border between heaven and earth. They are the warrior angels who fight against evil. They are the angels of birth and death.

> *For by Him all things were created that are in heaven and that are on earth, visible and invisible,*

whether thrones or dominions or principalities or powers. All things were created through Him and for Him. (Colossians 1:16)

Third Sphere of the Angels of God

The third sphere or specialty of the angels of God in heaven, are separated into three distinguished and specialized groups: the Principalities, Archangels, and Angels.

Principalities: These angels look over groups of people. They are in charge of the world's nations, cities, and towns. Their duties include taking charge of religion, politics, and the duties of angels on earth, below them.

For by Him all things were created that are in heaven and that are on earth, visible and invisible, whether thrones or dominions or principalities or powers. All things were created through Him and for Him. (Colossians 1:16)

Archangels: This is the chief angel, guardian of people and all things physical. The Archangel appears only in human form and has the task of being God's messenger to people at critical times of need.

For the Lord Himself will descend from heaven with a shout, with the voice of an archangel, and with the trumpet of God. And the dead in Christ will rise first. (1Thessalonians 4:16)

Angels: Throughout the Bible from Genesis to Revelation, these angels act as our personal guardians. They deliver prayers to God and return God's answer and messages to us. In my Christian life, I have experienced some of their activities and had several actual encounters with some of these angels. As a Christian, imagine how wonderful it would be to experience the magnificent of these angels and their activities in our lives because God has assigned them to us. Angels are the living beings God uses to send His messages to us and us to send Him messages, if we obey him and we use the Word of Christ.

> *And of the angels He says: "Who makes His angel spirits and His ministers a flame of fire" (Hebrews 1:7)*

Though one of the main characters of this book is Lucifer, I have chosen not to elaborate or recognize him much. Lucifer, is one of God's angels whom God created and held an important role in heaven, was to be God's lead worshiper. When Lucifer got sick of his life of service or assignments to God, he decided he wanted to rule the great Kingdom of heaven, rather than serving his Maker. Therefore, Lucifer attempted to take over the throne from God and fight his own Creator. In his attempt to do so, Lucifer convinced many other angels to join him.

As a result of Lucifer's disobedience in heaven, and his rebellion against God, he was forced out of heaven. This action resulted in the present situation where we now have angels of God and angels of Lucifer or satan. Everything God created was perfect. When God cast Lucifer out from heaven to separate him, because of his rebellion against God, Lucifer took one third of the angels in heaven with him. They are currently on earth and follow him to this present age, and will continue to do so until the final Day of Judgment. God has made it clear that He alone rules the Kingdom of heaven, a place of goodness, the paradise of paradises.

As a believer we must be able to recognize the activities of these two groups of angels (good angels and bad angels) in our lives. We know God sends His precious angels to mobilize his children for salvation. At the same time we must remember, that Lucifer mobilizes his own fallen angels to attack the children of God. For this reason, we must be familiar with the word of God and distinguish God's word from satan's word, when he speaks through his angels.

Lucifer's Rebellion and Consequences

Lucifer, the devil, is the enemy of the light bearer, of the Divine glory, an adversary of God, and a slanderer of His saints. He is an angel that has been known with different many names such as:

- **Lucifer** son of the morning (Isaiah 14:12)
- **Prince of darkness** and leviathan (Isaiah 27:1)
- **Beelzebub,** lord of flies or prince of demons (Matthew 12:24)
- **Father and Prince of lies** (John 8:44)
- **Satan,** the adversary (1Peter 5:8)
- **Dragon** (Revelation 12:9)
- **Old serpent** (Revelation12: 9)

- **Devil**, the accuser and slanderer (Revelation 12:10)

And war was broke out in heaven: Michael and his angels fought with the dragon; and the dragon and his angels fought, but they did not prevail, nor was a place found for them in heaven any longer. So the great dragon was cast out that serpent of old called the Devil and Satan, who deceives the whole world; he was cast to the earth, and his angels were cast out with him. (Revelation 12:7-9)

How you are fallen from heaven, O Lucifer, son of the morning! How you are cut down to the ground, You who weakened the nations! For you have said in your heart: 'I will ascend into heaven, I will exalt my throne above the stars of God; I will also sit on the mount of the congregation on the farthest sides of the north; I will ascend above the heights of the clouds, I will be like the Most High.' Yet you shall be brought down to Sheol, to the lowest depths of the Pit." (Isaiah 14:12-15)

We know from the creation that God created all His angels to serve and worship Him and God is not the creator of evil. By default we can say Lucifer who was also called, Son of the Morning, is the creator of all evil. Evil did not originate on earth, before God created the earth as He had already populated the universe with other rational beings. These beings are called

Angels. Angels are not creatures of fantasy or fake objects, they are simply another form of a living being that has come from the hands of God. The angels are not like mankind but they were created with a free-will like man, and were subject to the same conditions regarding their eternal life. At one point as it was in heaven, one of the most prominent of these angels chose to rebel against God and he failed in all his attempts.

In order to fully understand this book, we must first realize the conditions we live in today, and we are to determine, as best we can, which of the two entities or forces on the earth, are at work; the angels of God and angels of Lucifer. Which one are you listening to? Steady fellowship with the Word of God will determine which angel's activities appear in our lives. We also need to understand Lucifer as one of God's angels. Why did this once-prominent angel in heaven, became rebellious against God?

Lucifer became so infatuated with himself that he forgot that he was dependent on God for his very life. He was the most beautiful and brilliant angel in heaven and "*his heart was lifted up*" because he was so beautiful. Lucifer has not life in himself, however, He gets it from the same place humankind does and that is from GOD. He is also subject to God's judgment and will have no more power than we do to escape God's decision. From the beginning, God's creation of angels, including Lucifer, enjoyed certain benefits and privileges as loyal servants of God in heaven.

> *You were in Eden, the garden of God; Every precious stone was your covering: The sardius, topaz, and diamond, Beryl, onyx, and jasper,*

Sapphire, turquoise, and emerald with gold. The workmanship of your timbrels and pipes Was prepared for you on the day you were created. You were the anointed cherub who covers; I established you; You were on the holy mountain of God; You walked back and forth in the midst of fiery stones. (Ezekiel 28:13-14)

"By the abundance of your trading you became filled with violence within, And you sinned; Therefore, I cast you as a profane thing out of the mountain of God; And I destroyed you, O covering cherub, From the midst of the fiery stones. Your heart was lifted up because of your beauty; You corrupted your wisdom for the sake of your splendor; I cast you to the ground, I laid you before kings, that they might gaze at you. (Ezekiel 28:16-17)

Remember, the Lord did not create angels with the seed of sin in their heart, yet He gave them free will to serve Him.

You were perfect in your ways from the day you were created till iniquity was found in you. (Ezekiel 28:15)

We know that sin originated in the heart of Lucifer. We also know that God did not create sin because He created Lucifer. God created his creatures with the freedom of choice. Lucifer had the choice to remain loyal to God, or to rebel against his Creator.

Lucifer was created with no taint of maliciousness. His rebellion was not the fault of God, but as a result of his own choosing.

> *Let no one say when he is tempted, "I am tempted by God"; for God cannot be tempted by evil, nor does He Himself tempt anyone. But each one is tempted when he is drawn away by his own desires and enticed. (James 1:13-14)*

The reason that caused God's first creatures to rebel against Him, also continues to hold men and women in rebellion against God today.

> *"By the abundance of your trading you became filled with violence within, And you sinned; Therefore, I cast you as a profane thing out of the mountain of God; And I destroyed you, O covering cherub, From the midst of the fiery stones. Your heart was lifted up because of your beauty; You corrupted your wisdom for the sake of your splendor; I cast you to the ground, I laid you before kings, that they might gaze at you. (Ezekiel 28:16-17)*

The Lord has a final place of destruction, for Lucifer. He is the author of his own destruction. His intentional misuse of the gift of free will, a privilege given to him and all angels, will result in the bottomless pit.

41

"You defiled your sanctuaries by the multitude of your iniquities, By the iniquity of your trading; Therefore, I brought fire from your midst; It devoured you, And I turned you to ashes upon the earth in the sight of all who saw you. All who knew you among the peoples are astonished at you; you have become a horror, and shall be no more forever." (Ezekiel 28:18, 19)

Lord Jesus indicated to us that there are two sins originated from the heart of Lucifer and to those who follow him. He was a murderer without truth and a liar, because he is the <u>father of lies</u>.

The Lord said "You are of your father the devil, and the desires of your father you want to do. He was a murderer from the beginning, and does not stand in the truth, because there is no truth in him. When he speaks a lie, he speaks from his own resources, for he is a liar and the father of it. (John 8:44)

Lucifer remains a very destructive creature today, because of his intent and efforts to seize the throne of God, by force. A final place has been prepared, however, for him and his angels, where they will remain to eternity.

And war broke out in heaven: Michael and his angels fought with the dragon; and the dragon and his angels fought, but they did not prevail, nor was a place found for them in heaven any longer. So the great dragon was cast out, that serpent of old, called the Devil and Satan, who deceives the whole world; he was cast to the earth, and his angels were cast out with him. (Revelation 12:7-9)

The Bible tells us that stars symbolize angels, so when God cast satan out, he turned a third of God's angels against Him and brought these fallen angels with him.

His tail drew a third of the stars of heaven and threw them to the earth. And the dragon stood before the woman who was ready to give birth, to devour her Child as soon as it was born. (Revelation 12: 4)

Since his expulsion from heaven, Satan relentlessly seeks to deceive man whom God has created in His own image. Even though, the LORD forewarned Adam and Eve of the consequence of disobedience, Satan managed to seduce and entice the first woman to disregard God's warning and commandment. He disguised himself as a serpent and deceived the *first Woman on earth*. (Genesis 3:1-6)

The LORD created mankind as general overseers of earth. He gave them dominion over the fish of the sea, and over the fowl of the air, and every living thing that moves upon the earth. (Genesis1:28) The first man and woman created, gave their obedience to Satan. As a result, satan quickly seized the opportunity to take over the earth from them. From this act,

Satan was quick to proclaim his dominion over the earth. He has continued his war against God and mankind ever since. The Apostle Paul described him as the god of this world.

> *Whose minds the god of this age has blinded, who do not believe, lest the light of the gospel of the glory of Christ, who is the image of God, should shine on them. (2 Corinthians 4:4)*

God could have destroyed Satan immediately, when he rebelled against Him. God allowed satan, however, to demonstrate what the universe would be like under his authority. Today, we have seen in our world, the impact of his rebellion. God will take it over from him, when he completes his demonstration on earth. Satan is a defeated foe. He knows that soon he will be destroyed, and effects of his rebellion will be cleared from this world. He knows his end is near, so he desperately continues to fight against God. Sin has thoroughly perverted Satan's character, and he is beyond the point of no return, as far as repentance is concerned. Bitterness, hatred, and selfishness are the only roots that grow in satan's heart. He will intensify his hatred towards mankind, especially when men and women return to God and receive the forgiveness that he too, at one time, could have received.

> *"Therefore rejoice, O heavens, and you who dwell in them! Woe to the inhabitants of the earth and the sea! For the devil has come down to you, having great wrath, because he knows that he has a short time." (Revelation 12:12)*

Satan has used the fallen stars or the one-third of God's angels that came back to earth with him. He also has used the serpent, as the bible described to us, as the most cunning beast in the field.

> *Now the serpent was more cunning than any*
> *beast of the field which the LORD God had made.*
> *And he said to the woman Has God indeed said,*
> *you shall not eat of every tree of the garden?"*
> *(Genesis 3:1)*

One thing was certain, that Satan could not penetrate the mind of Christ in the wilderness, on earth, like he did to our first parents in the garden. According to scripture, Jesus was led up by the Spirit, into the wilderness, to be tempted by the devil. And when He had fasted forty days and nights, afterward He was hungry. Now when the tempter came to Him, he said, "*If You are the Son of God, command that these stones become bread.*" (Matthew 4:1-3) Satan came and proposed to Lord Jesus as he has done in the garden with Adam and Eve, but this time, he failed. He has afflicted many souls with sin and in all Satan's effort against God on earth, he still could not cause Jesus to sin against His Own Father in heaven. (Matthew 4:1-11)

> *"I will no longer talk much with you, for the ruler*
> *of this world is coming, and he has nothing in*
> *Me". (John 14:30)*

Another observation was that knowing surely that the event from the cross separates children of God from Satan permanently. This could only be achieved and sealed through the blood of Jesus Christ. Satan's disobedience and rebellion caused Jesus Christ's death on the cross. As a result, he not only lost his power over those he held captive in death, but also demonstrated the extent to which sin had corrupted him. Satan's selfish ambitions resulted in plans to murder the source of health and strength, for all mankind.

Moreover, Satan, the devil and his fallen angels manifested through the doctrine of demons by engaging in false teaching, another method to lure the children of God into darkness. According to Apostle Paul, in the last days, there would be segment of people that would give heed to "deceiving spirits and doctrines of demons." (1 Timothy 4:1) Therefore, the reality of demonic activity is more rampant than ever before. Scripture mentions demons forty-four times in the New Testament and only four times in the Old Testament. This is true because demons can also appear through teaching of wrong doctrine. Jesus Christ came and brought the truth to us on earth, but since He left, Satan and his followers began an aggressive campaign, questioning 'What is "Truth?' Thereby introducing his lies through the teaching of some churches and other religions. The origin of these demons was not clearly known or revealed, but they cannot be confused with the angels mentioned in 2 Peter 2:4.

> *For if God did not spare the angels who sinned,*
> *but cast them down to hell and delivered them*
> *into chains of darkness, to be reserved for judg-*
> *ment. (2 Peter 2:4)*

And the angels who did not keep their proper domain, but left their own abode, He has reserved in everlasting chains under darkness for the judgment of the great day (Jude 6.)

In discussing the role of the devil and his fallen angels, we must understand that in today's society, Satan and his angels appeared more often through the doctrine of teaching and prophecy, which contradict the Gospel of Jesus. What kind of teaching or prophecy are you hearing? Is he or she a false teacher or false prophet? Jesus gives a strong warning against the teaching false doctrine.

Nevertheless I have a few things against you, because you allow that woman Jezebel, who calls herself a prophetess, to teach and seduce My servants to commit sexual immorality and eat things sacrifice to idols. And I gave her time to repent of her sexual immorality, and she did not repent," Indeed I will cast her into a sickbed and those who commit adultery with her into great tribulation, unless they repent of their deeds. (Revelation 2:20-22)

Satan and his fallen angels have already been condemned to the bottomless pit. For those men and women who've decided in their hearts to listen and follow satan's doctrine of teaching and prophecy. There were warnings for them and they will be denied redemption by the blood. There is permanent judgment against them if they refuse to teach the Gospel of Christ and will be judged along with satan. There is hope though, and opportunity for those who are practicing these doctrines of demons, if they repent of their deeds. (Jude 6, Revelation 2:23)

I will kill her children with death, and all the churches shall know that I am He who searches the minds and hearts. And I will give to each one of you according to your works. (Revelation 2:23)

The Reality and Personality of Demons

1. Demons are spirit. "When unclean spirit goes out of a man, he goes through dry places, seeking rest, and finds none." (Matthew 12:43)
   "Then he goes and takes with him seven other spirits more wicked than himself and they enter and dwell there; and the last state of that man is worse than the first. So shall it *also be with this wicked generation.*" (Matthew 12:45)
2. Demons are satan's emissaries. If Satan casts out Satan, he is divided against himself. How then will this kingdom stand? And if I cast demons by Beelzebub, by whom do your sons cast them out? Therefore they shall be your judges. (Matthew 12:26-27)
3. Demons are ubiquitous. They are numerous as to make Satan's power practically ubiquitous (ever-present). *Then He asked to him, "What is your name?" And he answered, saying, "My name is Legion; for we are many."* (Mark 5:9)

4. Demons are capable of entering and controlling both men and animals. (Mark 5:2-5; 11-13) They desire and seek embodiment (incarnation), without which, apparently they are powerless for evil. (Matthew 12:43-44, Mark 5:10-12)

5. Demonic influence and demonic possession: They can be distinguished in the New Testament, (Matthew 4:24, 8:16, 28, 33; 9:32; 12:22; Mark 1:32; 5:15-16, 18; Luke 8:36; Acts 8:7; 16:16)

6. Demons are unclean, sullen, violent and malicious. (Matt 8:28, 9:33, 10:1 12:43; Mark 1:23, 5:3-5, 9:17, 20; Luke 6:18, 9:39.)

7. They know their eternal fate to be one of torment. (Matthew 8:29; Luke 8:31)

8. They inflict physical illness or maladies. However, mental illness is to be distinguished from a disorder of the mind due to demonic control. (Matthew 12:22, 17:15-18; Luke 13:16)

9. Demonic influence may manifest itself in various religions, by the nature of its severity, asceticism or somberness. They have tendencies to degenerate into uncleanness. (1Timothy 4:1-3)

10. A clear sign of demonic influence in religion is a departure from the faith, revealed in scripture. (1Timothy 4:1)

11. Demons maintain a conflict with Christians who would be spiritual. (Ephesians 6:12; 1Timothy 4:1-3) The Christian's resources are prayer and bodily control. (Matthew 17:21) The whole armor of God must be in place to fight. (Ephesians 6:13-14)

12. All unbelievers are open to demon possession. In which you once walked according to the course of this world, according to the prince of the power of the air, the spirit who now works in the sons of disobedience. (Ephesians 2:2).

13. Exorcism in the name of Jesus Christ was practiced for demon possession. And this she did for many days. But Paul, greatly annoyed, turned and said to the spirit, "I command you in the name of Jesus Christ to come out of her." And he came out that very hour. (Acts 16:18)

14. One awful feature of the apocalyptic judgment in this age is the emergence of demons out of the bottomless pit. (Revelation 9:1-11, 20)

15. Jesus Christ is known to satan and demons, as the Most High God. They recognize His Supreme Authority. (Mark 1:23-24; Luke 6:18, 9:39) So the demons begged Him, saying, "If you cast us out, permit us to go away" into the herd of swine. And He said to them. "Go." So when they had come out, they went into the herd of swine. And suddenly the whole herd of swine ran violently down the steep place into the sea, and perished in the water. (Matthew 8:31-32)

Heaven is the throne of God. Earth is the place for man to rule and hell is the place for satan to rule. Who you obey now, determines your master and whom you will worship.

GOD AND HIS CREATIONS

He has made the earth by His power; He has established the world by His wisdom, And stretched out the heaven by His understanding. (Jeremiah 51:15)

Jehovah Elohim, Lord GOD created the heavens and earth and all things in them. The first chapter of Genesis explains how God created all the great things on earth and the second chapter describes the creation of man, woman and the garden, in which he placed them to dwell in. Everything He created was perfect, good and pure. All good things come from above, God. Therefore, think good of Him always.

Thus, the heavens and the earth, and all the host of them were finished. And on the seventh day God completed His work, and He rested on the seventh day from all His work. Then God blessed the seventh day and sanctified it, because in it He rested from all His work He had made. (Genesis 2:1-3)

Creation of Nature

The earth was not yet formed or cultivated with plants of the field or herbs, because man was not yet on the earth to cultivate them or enjoy them. The earth was completely covered by water and there was no need to rain on earth, at that time. The LORD watered the land with dew and mist that came up from the earth. The original earth that God created was quite different from today. Today, the earth is watered by rain from heaven and different areas experience contrasting weather patterns, making some areas arid and others wet.

On the second day of God's creation, after he had created light on the first day, He created a big reservoir in the heavens, the vapor above, then formed water below on earth. Then God said, Let there be a firmament in the midst of the waters and let it divide the waters from the waters. (Genesis 2:6-7) It remained this way until God, opened His living fountains of water from heaven, and rain fell on the earth for the first time, during the great flood of Noah. There was no need for rain earth until sin gripped man totally and God couldn't stand it any longer. So He used His fountains of waters to flush out the iniquity of man on earth; the exception being Noah, his family and the selected animals. Two serpents were also kept in the ark, among the other animals, as the Lord had instructed Noah.

Creation of Man

Man and woman were formed last among the living creatures made by God. First God created man's body from the dust, and all things were in place, but there was no life in him. God is the source of life, so He created man's heart and lungs, and man became a living being with flesh, after He had breathed into man, the breath of life. God is Spirit so He breathed His Spirit into man and Adam became the son of God on the earth.

> *The LORD formed man from the dust of the ground and breathed into his nostrils and man became a living being. (Genesis 2:7)*

The naming of all the animals did not occur until after the man was created. God created man and had created a comfortable place for man to live, the Garden of Eden. The LORD planted a garden eastward in Eden and put the man whom He had formed, to be in-charge.

> *And out of the ground the LORD God made every tree grow that is pleasant to the sight and good for food. The tree of life was also in the midst of the garden, and the tree of the knowledge and of good and evil. (Genesis 2:8-9)*

The garden was beautiful to look upon and there was good food. This shows the caring God we have, who thinks of things that will delight and be pleasant to His children. I often wonder if this may be one of the reasons Lucifer is jealous of man. The angels were not created with same splendor, He had offered to man. Man started his test of obedience probably from the beginning, when the LORD placed man in the eastward garden, where the tree of life and the tree of knowledge of good and evil. (Genesis 2:8-9)

In the midst of the garden, God placed the tree of knowledge of good and evil. One of the adages of old folks is, "What you will not eat, don't put in your nose to smell it." An example of this is the tree of knowledge of good and evil, planted, in the center of the garden; but God had earlier warned man not to eat of it, otherwise he would die. As His children, it's a sober reminder that we must always adhere to His instructions, rather than following what we see. We must listen to what He is saying, do what we are hearing and be obedient to his instruction.

Everything man needed was provided for them eastward of the garden, where He placed him. This garden was watered by a river, which originated from Eden. This main river from Eden, divided into four separate riverheads called the Phison, the Gihon, the Hiddekel and the Euphrates. This area of the garden must have been quite large, as each of these rivers watered named lands such as Havilah, which contain gold and precious stones (Bdellium and Onyx). Gihon the second river goes around the entire land of Cush. Hidddekel the third river goes east toward Assyria, while the fourth river is the Euphrates. Today, we cannot geographically trace or indicate the Garden of Eden. (Genesis 2:10-14)

> *Then the LORD God took the man and put him in the Garden of Eden to tend and keep it. (Genesis 2:15)*

Whatever God gave to man he wanted them to be responsible for it. The garden needed pruning, dressing and keeping.

54

This was the occupation the LORD first gave to man; to culti-vate the garden and be sustained by it. From the beginning, man was given a purpose in life. Today, man's purpose is still to be productive in providing management of the garden. The garden now is the earth we are living in today.

Do you know why you are here or why you are created? Everyone has an assignment to do on earth. What is yours? And if you do not know His will concerning you, seek His face to find out. Do not allow strangers or satan to change that assignment, like he did to our first parents, Adam and Eve.

Creation of Animals

God told man the do's and don'ts of the kingdom which He built for them, in the Garden of Eden. He told them, every tree of the garden you may eat, but you must stay away from the tree of the knowledge of good and evil, for the day you eat of it, you will die. (Genesis 2:17) The angels, including Lucifer, were already formed. Satan, also called Lucifer, was standing and watching all God's creation, that were made after him, step by step. God had already created the angels long before He created Adam. (Genesis 2:19)

The LORD created animals as helpers for man, so that he will not be alone in the garden. He also created a helper com-parable to him. As the LORD created man from the ground, He also formed from the ground, every beast of the field and every bird of the air; and brought them to Adam to see what he would call them. Whatever Adam called each of this living creatures, so will be their name. Even though the LORD cre-ated these living creatures as helpers to Adam, these animals

55

were not found to be comparable to Adam. The LORD God did not create animals in his own image. He formed them from the ground but did not breathe into their nostrils, like He did with Adam.

Adam called the name of each animal one by one as he desired. As a result, these animals bear and take upon the behavior and characteristics of that animal's name. When He called an animal's name it quickly took up the behavior of such animal. When He called the horse, the animal behaved like a horse and not like a cow. When He called the eagle, the eagle flew higher than any other bird. When He called the whale, it immediately took up the behavior of a big fish in the ocean, residing only in water. (Genesis 2:19, 20)

When Adam called to name the snake, serpent, it quickly took up the behavior and characteristics of a snake, not as a spider or millipede or any other crawling or creeping creature. According to scripture we were told that the snake also is the most cunning beast of the field, more cunning than any other living creature. (Genesis 3:1a) Thus, the lion, cat, leopard, horse, parrot or any other animal, was not cunning like the snake. There were tens of thousands of animal species at the garden with Adam, and many of these animals still exist around the world today. In fact, these animals were formed to help Adam.

From inception, Lucifer watched God as he made each creature on earth inside the Garden of Eden, the creation of man and animals through creation of the woman. Lucifer was one of the lead angels of God in heaven, before his disobedience and rebellion. He was created to serve and worship his Creator forever. He is the serpent of old, also called satan.

Since God cast Lucifer out of heaven to earth, he has been roaming and rebelling against God, the Creator. Lucifer saw and noted when Adam named the snake, that it is the most cunning beast in the field. He continued to watch God's creations.

Creation of Woman

The creation of the woman did not occur until after God created nature, animals and man. The Lord said let Us create man in Our image and then they created the first man on the earth. Adam was created first. The creation of the first man on earth without the woman, was an indication of the importance of mankind to God and God's attention to man, was unlike any other of His prior creations. The LORD then created a wife for Adam.

Amazingly, in His creation of plants and animals, since the beginning, the LORD created them male and female, so that each can reproduce after it's own kind. From man, God created woman. Man by himself was incomplete, because he did not have a companion. He made plants and animals both male and female. Then the Lord did not want man to be alone, so He created the woman from the man's rib. The purpose of woman was birthed and the Lord put Adam to sleep and took one of his ribs to make a woman to be his helper. Everything on the earth, both plants and animals reproduce its own kind, so man also needed a woman to reproduce their own kind.

> *And the LORD caused a deep sleep to fall on Adam, and he slept, and He took one of his ribs and closed up the flesh in its place. Then the*

rib in which the LORD had taken from man, He made into a woman, and He brought her to the man. (Genesis 2:21, 22.)

The LORD created a helper for man. This tells me often that God knows what we need before we're even born. Before we even think about what we need, He's already made provision for us.

Adam said, "This now bone of my bones and flesh of my flesh; She shall be called Woman, because she was taken out of Man." (Genesis 2:23)

After God brought the first woman created to help Adam, he saw that this woman looked like him, and quite different from the thousands of the animals that he had previously named. Adam knew that the woman's flesh and bone structures were very similar to his own, that is why he called the woman bone of his bones and flesh of his flesh. Scripture reveals how God instituted the first marriage on earth, when Adam met his wife. God's original plan in the beginning was man and woman working together with a common goal and purpose in life. God's plan was for male and female to be together, so they can reproduce according to their likeness.

Therefore, a man shall leave his father and mother and be joined to his wife, and they shall become one flesh. And they were both naked, the man and his wife, and were not ashamed. (Genesis 2:24-25)

Adam did not name his wife but called her "Woman", that is female. Adam's wife did not have her name, Eve, until after they were deceived, by the serpent, in the garden; and the LORD punished them. Man's disobedience to God's word came about because the serpent deceived Eve.

> *And Adam was not deceived, but the woman being deceived, fell into transgression. (1 Timothy 2:14)*

After God rendered his punishment against man, Adam finally called his wife and named her Eve, because she was the mother of all humanity. Then the LORD made Adam and his wife Eve tunics of skin and clothed them. God said because man had become like one of Us, by eating from the tree of knowledge to know good and evil, they will be sent out from the Garden of Eden, to till the ground.

As a result, our world today is rebellious, perverted and is gradually changing from the original purpose God has for mankind on the earth. Lucifer continues his acts of disobedience and rebellion; to seduce men and women to deviate from the primary purpose, for which they were created.

CHAPTER THREE

DON'T BLAME WOMEN

"She was not at the Naming Ceremony"

Both sexes have blamed women for the fault of men. Men and women blamed Eve for the fall of man, in the Garden of Eden. So we all have accused, brought to court and prosecuted, Eve, the first woman. This constituted the title of this book. Now we are rediscovering the first woman's impeachment. We understand that the first woman was impeached, meaning, accused.

So as you read this book, you'll realize that we have been blaming the wrong person for a long time. For example, a young child who is crawling does not know how to climb the steps, when that child falls down the steps, do you take the child to court? The blind man was crossing the road and a car was coming and the car moved to avoid hitting the man, but he hits another truck instead. Do you then take the blind man to court? You cannot blame somebody who is ignorant of a missing piece of information. The serpent knew when God created woman, but the woman did not know when the serpent, or Lucifer, was created. On the other hand, the serpent witnessed the creations of God, even though he was separated from heaven.

God Created Woman after Animals

All the beasts on the earth were created before God created the woman as a female companion for Adam. The first woman created was not there at the naming ceremony of these animals. As a result of the woman being created last, she does not have knowledge of the behavior and characteristics of any of these animals that her husband named.

Satan Tempted the Woman

Various perspectives have been given to explain this ancient unanswered question. Why did satan tempt the woman and not Adam? Understanding the order of creation and the preceding events that occurred in heaven, which resulted in God casting out one of His outstanding angels from heaven, will shed some light. God is of order. Before he created certain things he already knew what it would look like.

When God put Adam and the woman in the Garden of Eden, they were both perfect and innocent. They obeyed God in all things as He commanded them, until the enemy satan, came to talk with Eve. Pride is the root of all evil and it all started from heaven. How can pride possibly originate in heaven? Lucifer got jealous of his creator and pride got a hold of him, which is when he began to campaign and wage a war against God and

His angels. The throne of God was attractive to Lucifer, so he wanted the throne, forgetting that it was God who created him.

Lucifer re-named satan, assaulted our first parents by drawing them to sin by disobeying God, and the temptation proved fatal to them. Satan, the devil was the tempter, in the shape and likeness of a Serpent. Satan's plan was to separate man from God, since he himself had been cast out from heaven. The person tempted was the woman. It was satan's desire and strategy to converse with the woman when she was alone, even though her husband was around. Satan knew the behaviors and characteristics of all the animals, which God created and asked Adam to name. He then searched through his scheme of strategies and found that it was most appropriate for him to take the likeness of a snake, the serpent, in disguise when approaching the woman.

Snake, the Serpent is the most cunning, shrewd, crafty and devious animal in the field according to Genesis 3:1

Remember that the angels of God were the first of God's creatures and they are very special. They handle certain things which man cannot handle, because of the way God created them. Man on the other hand was created in God's likeness. Then, the Creator breathed into Adam's nostrils, which made him unique and different from any other of God's creation on earth. God did not create angels, animals, or any other creature, in His image, as he had done with humans. Therefore, men are peculiar, as man was made in the likeness of God, to serve Him and have dominion over every other living creature on earth, below and above.

> *For You have made him a little lower than the angels, And You have crowned him with glory and honor. (Psalm 8:5)*

> *You have made him a little lower than the angels; You have crowned him with glory and honor, And set him over the works of Your hands. (Hebrews 2:7)*

> *But we see Jesus, who was made a little lower than the angels, for the suffering of death crowned with glory and honor, that He, by the grace of God, might taste death for everyone. (Hebrews 2:9)*

Satan knew well enough, the only possible way for him to get back at God is to attack the man, Adam, through his wife, the first woman.

Therefore, satan sought out his own knowledge of creation, to determine which animal would be most appropriate and susceptible for him to enter and possess, thereby disguising himself before the woman. So, satan acquired the serpent's appearance, behavior and characteristics. Even today, when someone's behavior isn't quite normal, we have a tendency to call such person an animal, saying '*He is an animal!*'

Lucifer new Adam was God's first son and he also knew that God created Adam in his own image. Satan knew also that Adam named all the animals one by one, as the LORD God inspired and presented them to him. He named them all. Therefore as fallen stars, satan knew that Adam had power over all animals as God had commanded him. Have dominion over all things on the earth, above and below. (Genesis 1:26) Satan did not go to tempt Adam directly, because Adam named the serpent and Adam knew the behavior and characteristics of the snake. Adam knew the serpent was the most cunning beast in the field.

During the naming ceremony of these wonderful animals, that LORD God had formed from the ground, Adam had full knowledge of all animal behaviors as the LORD had inspired him to name them. The behavior and characteristics of each animal appeared when he called their name one by one. The breath of God comes out from Adam's mouth, each time he speaks and called the name of these animals. Therefore, I am convinced that Adam knew the serpent as the most cunning or crafty beast of the field. The serpent did not go to Adam directly because Adam knew the behavior of a serpent. The only option left for satan, is to disguise himself as the serpent and go to Adam's wife by making the fatal inquiry about the tree, in the garden. Why? She wasn't aware of the behavior of a serpent.

Serpent's Strategy against Mankind

The man was not tempted by evil, but by his wife, Eve. She had taken the forbidden fruit from the tree of the knowledge, which the LORD had warned, not to eat or touch. She gave some to Adam, who ate it.

So when the woman saw that the tree was good for food, that it was pleasant to the eyes, and a tree desirable to make one wise, she took of its fruit and ate. She also gave to her husband and he ate. Then the eyes of both of them were opened, and they knew that they were naked; and they sewed fig leaves together and made themselves coverings. (Genesis 3:6-7)

This first sin brought death to humanity. Adam and Eve were sent out of the Garden of Eden because of their obedience to satan and disobedience to their Creator. Then God placed the angel Cherubim with a flaming sword to guard the tree of life while he sent Adam and Eve out of the Garden of Eden.

Therefore the Lord God sent him out of the garden of Eden to till the ground from which he was taken. So He drove out the man; and He placed cherubim at the east of the garden of Eden, and a flaming sword which turned every way, to guard the way to the tree of life. (Genesis 3:23-24)

Satan took advantage of this innocent woman's vulnerability and disguised himself in order to deceive her, because of her ignorance. (Genesis 3:5-6) Unfortunately Adam probably did not finish telling his spouse about all God's creation. Scripture, however, reveals Eve knew which fruit of the garden they could and could not eat.

"Has God indeed (certainly or undeniably), said you shall not eat of every tree of the garden?" (Genesis 3:1b)

The serpent was making a mockery of God's word to the children of God. The serpent inquired of the woman, *"Has God indeed said that you shall not eat of every tree of the garden?"* (Genesis 3:1)

The answer should have been yes, no, or ignore the serpent. Many times while the enemy is talking, we pay too much attention to his whispers, innuendos, suggestions, and false advice. Anytime you engage in conversation too long with a stranger or enemy, the consequence is sometimes horrible and deadly.

Who is the serpent that has been watching and following you and your family members? Is he residing in the workplace? Parties? Friends or relatives? As a result, many people get distracted in life because of a stranger's voice they've listened to and it has remained with them. Sometimes that stranger's voice will follow them everywhere they go and eventually leading them to an inappropriate journey in life, leading to destruction.

But he who enters by the door is the shepherd of the sheep. And when he brings out his own sheep, he goes before them; and the sheep follow him for they know his voice. (John 10:4)

Yet they will by no means follow a stranger, but will flee from him, for they do not know the voice of strangers. (John 10:5)

I am the good shepherd' and I know My sheep, and am known by My own. (John 10:14)

My sheep hear My voice, and I know them, and they follow Me. And I give them eternal life and they shall never perish; neither shall anyone snatch them out of My hand. (John 10:27-28)

The serpent knew who he was talking with, but the woman did not know what she was getting herself into. The woman didn't know the serpent is the most cunning or crafty beast of the field. The conversation had gone on too long between them, especially for her. Ignorance can sometimes be like a disease, as what you don't know can destroy you. Adam's wife didn't know this fallen angel, satan, had already rebelled against God in heaven. Nor did she understand his primary agenda is to attack God and his children on earth, till the end of age.

How you are fallen from heaven, O Lucifer, son of the morning! How you are cut down to the ground, You who weakened the nations! For you have said in your heart: I will ascend into heaven, I will exalt my throne above the stars of God; I will also sit on the mount of the congregation On the farthest sides of the north; I will ascend above the heights of the clouds, I will be like the Most High.' Yet you shall be brought down to Sheol, To the lowest depths of the Pit. (Isaiah 14:12-15)

> *Those who see you will gaze at you, And con-*
> *sider you, saying: is this the man who made*
> *the earth tremble, Who shook kingdoms Who*
> *made the world as a wilderness And destroyed*
> *its cities, Who did not open the house of his pris-*
> *oners?" (Isaiah 14:16-17)*

This innocent woman went a little further by talking to the stranger about her life and where she lives, her husband's name and location down the street, how many children she will have, what they can eat in their house and what they cannot not eat. You get my drift. The first woman had given too much information and detail to the stranger. The serpent did not ask Eve all the information she was providing; she volunteered that information to the devil.

> *The Woman said to the serpent "We may eat*
> *the fruit of the trees of the garden, but of the fruit*
> *of the tree which is in the midst of the garden,*
> *God has said, "You shall not eat it, nor shall you*
> *touch it, lest you die. (Genesis 3:2-3)*

The information was given only to Adam and Eve, not the angels. Through the years, we've often seen illustrations of the woman actually near the forbidden fruit, when she spoke with satan. So people ascertain, she wouldn't have been tempted if she wasn't near the forbidden tree. That's why satan took advantage of her. Yet I'd like to challenge conventional thinking and state that she wasn't near the tree. If she was near the tree she probably would have replied to satan by saying, here is the tree or the tree is over there. That was not how she replied to satan, instead she said,

> *"We may eat the fruit of the trees of the garden,*
> *but of the fruit of the tree which is in the midst of*
> *the garden;" (Genesis 3:2b)*

It is the craftiness of Satan to speak of the divine law as uncertain or unreasonable to draw people to sin. It is our wisdom to keep a firm belief in God's commandments, ordinances and decrees with a high respect for each.

Satan was actually trying to find out which tree in the midst of the garden they should not eat. There are many trees that bear all kinds of different fruits in the garden. Satan did not know the particular tree that will cause man to fall short before God. When God created Adam and Eve, He breathed into their nostrils the breath of life and man became a living being. (Genesis 2:7) He released the language of Heaven; the Holy Spirit, to them through His Spirit. The language God spoke to them was in the Holy Spirit language, as God is Spirit. Satan does not understand the Holy Spirit language. *For he who speaks in a tongue does not speak to men but to God for no one understands him; however, in the spirit he speaks mysteries.* (1Corinthians 14:2) This is why as a believer, you should be encouraged and patiently ask God to give you His language of the Holy Spirit, which enables us to speak mysteries to God.

> *But you, beloved, building yourselves up on*
> *your most holy faith, praying in the Holy Spirit.*
> *(Jude 1:20)*

When you speak this language, not only do you speak mysteries, you are speaking directly and only, to the Almighty God. Satan does not understand the language of heaven.

For he who speaks in tongue does not speak to men but to God, for no one understands him; however in the spirit he speaks mysteries. (1Corithians 14:2)

I encourage you to desire it and ask God to anoint your tongue to speak His heavenly language.

Don't blame the woman, because the woman didn't know the character and behavior of the serpent. She was too busy enjoying God's creation in the Garden of Eden. Scriptures advises us also: *"lest Satan should take advantage of us; for we are not ignorant of his devices."* (2 Corinthians 2:11)

The enemy's primary goal, since God cast him out of heaven, is to steal, kill and destroy. As satan knows where he belongs at the end of this age. Scripture says:

The thief does not come except to steal, and to kill, and to destroy. I have come that they may have life, and that they may have it more abundantly. (John 10:10)

Eve said to the serpent, we may eat the fruit of the garden, but not the one in midst of the garden. Then Eve told the serpent if they do otherwise, that is touch or eat the fruit they will die. Satan now got a full measure of understanding. He was after their lives, so Eve made it easy for him. His goal towards mankind is to steal, kill and destroy. Now satan knew the exact fruit of the tree of garden that he could entice them to eat.

> *Then the serpent said to the woman, "You will not surely die. For God knows that in the day you eat of it your eyes will be opened, and you will be like God, knowing good and evil." (Genesis 3:4-5)*

God sent man out from the Garden of Eden, which was a replica of heaven on earth, until the Day of Judgment. Fortunately, mankind will have a second opportunity, because the LORD God has sent His Beloved Son, Jesus Christ, to redeem man from all their sins, by shedding His blood on the cross.

> *But now in Christ Jesus you who once were far off have been brought near by the blood of Christ (Ephesians 2:13).*

Kingdom of Light and Darkness at War

There are two kingdoms fighting constantly right here on the earth, the Kingdom of God in heaven and the kingdom of darkness from below. And from the days of John the Baptist until now, the kingdom of heaven suffers violence, and the violent take it by force. (Matthew 11:12) God created Adam and Eve from the ground and breathed His Holy Spirit into them. Man was filled with the Spirit of God until the enemy came to entice and corrupt them. Since then, the Devil filled with wrath, has brought evil to humanity.

> *Then I saw an angel coming down from heaven, having the key to the bottomless pit and a great chain in his hand. (Revelation 20:1)*

> *He laid hold of the dragon, that serpent of old, who is the Devil and Satan, and bound him for a thousand years. (Revelation 20:2)*

> *And he cast him into the bottomless pit, shut him up, and set a seal on him. So that he should deceive the nations no more till the thousand years were finished. But after these things he must be released for a little while. (Revelation 20:3)*

Even though it was Eve's weakness to engage in wrong conversation with the serpent, she might have perceived his question wrongly, based on the answer she gave him. Satan's goal was to teach men first to doubt, deny God and then finally point their finger at God, for what He has deprived His children.

Therefore, let us resist the devil and evil will flee from us. Satan, purposed in his heart to confuse Adam and Eve and to be discontent with the benefits, God offered them in the garden. God gave them dominion over all things on earth, above and below, plus the gift to live forever.

Therefore, always think well of God as the Good Father you have, and then think ill of sin, as evil on the earth. Let us resist the devil, and he will flee from us.

> *Therefore submit to God. Resist the devil and he will flee from you. (James 6:7)*

CHAPTER FOUR

FIRST WOMAN IMPEACHED

Re-discovering of the first woman impeached.

On the sixth day of the creation, God created man in His likeness and in the image of God He created him, male and female, He created them. Then He blessed them to be fruitful and multiply, fill the earth and subdue it. He told the man to have dominion over the earth forever. Everything God had created on earth was perfect and glorious. God knows the end of all things from the beginning. He is omnipotent. The creator did not plant evil on the land, but evil cropped up from the ground.

The most innocent first lady of all time was impeached, because she was ignorant of the devices of the enemy. The fight was between God and Satan.

Who is Lucifer or Satan, the Devil? *(Accuser of the Brethren)*

Therefore, let us examine the character, knowledge and behavior of this evil man in his attempt to destroy humanity. He is cunning and crafty and has a countless number of schemes in his repertoire. Do you know Lucifer, the Devil?

> *I will ascend above the heights of the clouds, I will be like the Most High.' Yet you shall be brought down to Sheol, To the lowest depths of the Pit. (Isaiah 14:14-15)*

1. Lucifer, the Daystar bright one (Isaiah 14:12)
2. Devil, the accuser and slanderer (Revelation 12:10)
3. Satan, the adversary (1Peter 5:8)
4. Dragon, indicating his power (Revelation 12:9)
5. Beelzebub, the lord of flies and prince of demons (Matthew 12:24)
6. The Old Serpent (Revelation12:9)
7. The father and prince of lies (John 8:44)
8. The Prince of Darkness and leviathan. (Isaiah 27:1)
9. Satan's goal is to have someone focus on themselves rather than God (Genesis 3:4-5)
10. Satan tempts humanity with his ways rather than God's ways. (Genesis 3:6-7)
11. Lucifer is here on earth to steal, kill and destroy. (John 10:10)

Who is Eve, Adam's wife? (The first woman impeached)

Eve was perfect and had no sin or evil within her when God brought her to her husband, Adam. Generations of men and women today, come from our first earthly parents, Adam and Eve. So, who is the real Eve? The woman the world has been talking about since the fall of man, in Genesis chapter three. She was created in God's image and bore the breath of God in her until she was polluted and contaminated, by eating from the wrong fruit tree, in the Garden of Eden.

What happened in the garden set the precedent to what's happening in our lives today. The first accuser of the brethren is Satan, the devil. Men always point fingers at the woman, but let's delve into how sin started in the beginning, with Satan. When God asked Adam,

> *"Who told you that you were naked? Have you eaten from the tree of which I commanded you that you should not eat?"*
>
> *Then the man said, "The woman whom You gave to be with me, she gave me of the tree and I ate." (Genesis 3:11, 12)*

Both men and women continue to accuse the woman as the cause of the fall of man, in the Garden of Eden. Let us examine what scripture says, when Satan was making his inquiry from Eve.

I. Whoever is interrogating you does matter.
(Accuser and cross-examiner)

The serpent suddenly appeared to the woman and engaged in the interrogation with this innocent woman. The only one we ought to answer to is God, never the enemy. So, it is of vital importance to be able to discern with whom you are speaking, listening to and obeying. Satan doesn't have full information about our lives, so he accuses or pokes into your lives anytime he wants to gain access to more information about us. What are you telling him? Fast forward to Jesus, who knew satan's ways and said, *"Get behind me, satan!..."* (Matthew 16:23) In another instance, *Jesus answered and said to him, "Get behind Me, satan! For it is written, 'You shall worship the Lord your God, and Him only you shall serve.'"* (Luke 4:8)

Often people often come to us to gain information in order to complete a case that they haven't fully developed in their mind, which they plan to use against us, eventually. Guard information about yourself.

> He said to the woman, <u>Has God indeed said,</u> *"You shall not eat every tree of the garden. (Genesis 3:1b)*

> And the woman said to the serpent, "We may eat fruit of the trees of the garden. But of the fruit of the tree which is <u>in the midst</u> of the garden, God has said, 'You shall not eat it, nor shall you touch it, lest you die.'" (Genesis 3:3)

II. What information does the enemy need from you?
(Evil Inquiry)

The importance of guarding information about ourselves reminds me of the story of King Hezekiah, who invited his enemy to his palace and showed them all his belongings.

Hezekiah exposed his wealth and instruments of defense to the Babylonian embassy:

> *And Hezekiah was attentive to them, and showed them all the house of his treasures—the silver and gold, the spices and precious ointment, and all his armory—all that was found among his treasures. There was nothing in his house or in all his dominion that Hezekiah did not show them. Then Isaiah the prophet went to King Hezekiah, and said to him, "What did these men say, and from where did they come to you?" So Hezekiah said, "They came from a far country, from Babylon." And he said, "What have they seen in your house?" So Hezekiah answered, "They have seen all that is in my house; there is nothing among my treasures that I have not shown them." (2 Kings 20:13-15)*

> *Then Isaiah said to Hezekiah, "Hear the word of the Lord: 'Behold, the days are coming when all that is in your house, and what your fathers have accumulated until this day, shall be carried to Babylon; nothing shall be left,' says the Lord. 'And they shall take away some of your sons who will descend from you, whom you will beget; and they shall be eunuchs in the palace of the king of Babylon.'" (2 Kings 20:16-18)*

So Hezekiah said to Isaiah, "The word of the Lord which you have spoken is good!" For he said, "Will there not be peace and truth at least in my days?" Now the rest of the acts of Hezekiah— all his might, and how he made a pool and a tunnel and brought water into the city—are they not written in the book of the chronicles of the kings of Judah? (2 Kings 20:19-20)

III. What information are you sharing with your enemy?

Giving too much information can be deadly. The woman disclosed too much information about herself, to the serpent, pointing satan to the exact location of the tree, which God had forbidden them to eat from. (Genesis 3:2-3)

*And the woman said to the serpent, "We may eat fruit of the trees of the garden but of the fruit of the tree which is in the **midst of the garden**, God has said, 'You shall not eat it, nor shall you touch it, lest you die.'" (Genesis 3:2, 3)*

IV. What information have you received from God?

The LORD told Adam and his wife which fruit they should eat and the fruit they should not eat. How many times have you heard from God, and someone comes afterward trying to convince you otherwise? The Lord had given Adam and his wife everlasting life, when he created them and placed them in the Garden of Eden. Satan came afterwards, to give man death. Any time you pay attention to what God is telling you, you are guaranteed a blissful life. If you do not know His voice or ways yet, begin to spend more time in the Word and He will reveal more to you.

> *Then God blessed them, and God said to them, Be fruitful and multiply; fill the earth and subdue it; have dominion over the fish of the sea, over the birds of the air and over every living thing that moves on the earth. (Genesis 2:18)*

V. Who is making you focus on yourself, rather than the Creator?

Satan made the first parents to re-focus on themselves rather than God. Any time your focus shifts from God to yourself, you are listening to the stranger within you. The father of lies enticed, seduced, induced and deceived Eve and transgressed Adam, to believe that they would not die if they ate the forbidden fruit. Instead, he told them their eyes would be opened and they will be like God, knowing good and evil. He lied and manipulated them to buy into his game. Which one of his games have you experienced lately?

> *Then the serpent said to the woman, You will not surely die. For God knows that in the day you eat of it your eyes will be opened, and you be like God, knowing good and evil. (Genesis 3:4-5)*

VI. What advice have you received from the satan?

Satan's advice is deadly and we must flee from him. His recommendations about anything are like deadly chemicals injected into a person's bloodstream. Yes, it's that serious. Satan presents his advice when you haven't asked for any. He'll come voluntarily, in a loud or sometimes in a gentle voice(s) to make suggestions. If satan will try to tempt Jesus, he will tempt anyone.

> *Then Jesus was led up by the Spirit into the wilderness to be tempted by the devil. And when He had fasted forty days and forty nights, afterward He was hungry. Now when the tempter came to Him, he said, "If You are the Son of God, command that these stones become bread." But He answered and said, "It is written, 'Man shall not live by bread alone, but by every word that proceeds from the mouth of God.'" (Matthew 4:1-4)*

> *Then the devil took Him up into the holy city, set Him on the pinnacle of the temple, and said to Him, "If You are the Son of God, throw Yourself down. For it is written: 'He shall give His angels charge over you,' and, 'In their hands they shall bear you up, Lest you dash your foot against a stone.'" Jesus said to him, "It is written again, 'You shall not tempt the Lord your God.'" (Matthew 4:5-7)*

> *Again, the devil took Him up on an exceedingly high mountain, and showed Him all the kingdoms of the world and their glory. And he said to Him, "All these things I will give You if You will fall down and worship me." Then Jesus said to him, "Away with you, Satan! For it is written, 'You shall worship the Lord your God, and Him only you shall serve. (Matthew 4:8-10)*

His advice or recommendations always lead to his intended result, which is to steal, kill and destroy. All evil comes from him and nothing good comes from satan and his agents. Carefully consider who is making suggestions on what you should do or not do? It might be satan.

I often liken satan's advice to snake venom. Once snake venom is released into a person's blood stream after being bitten, the victim becomes very weak and tired, finding it difficult to get away. Anytime someone speaks into your life and by the time you've left, you feel weak, tired, discouraged or anxious you may have just have received a dose of the serpent's poison.

> *Then the serpent said to the woman, "You will not surely die, for God knows that in the day, you eat of it your eyes will be opened, and you will be like God, knowing good and evil. (Genesis 3:4, 5)*

VII. What language are you speaking to your situation?

When God created Adam and his wife, there was only one language, it is the language of truth and holiness. It's the language of heaven, called the language of the Holy Spirit. When satan was cast down to earth, he developed his own language, which is considered to be the language of deceit and lies. When God speaks, He speaks truth and holiness. His language came from His breath in holiness and righteousness. Therefore when He gave instructions about the garden, He spoke in the language of truth and holiness with them, in the garden. He always tells His children what He wants them to do and what He expects from them. Scripture says, *Surely, the Lord God does nothing unless He reveals His secrets to His servants the prophets.* (Amos 3:7) God doesn't go back and forth like satan does. God values His word more than His name. Therefore, today plant the seed of God into your situation. According to the parable of Jesus, *"the seed is the word of God".* (Luke 8:11)

> *Then God blessed them, and God said to them,*
> *"Be fruitful and multiply; fill the earth and subdue*
> *it; have dominion over the fish of the sea, over*
> *the birds of the air, and over every living thing*
> *that moves on the earth." (Genesis 1: 28.)*

The heavenly language has remained a mystery to mankind and especially to your enemy. God gave all instructions in the garden to His children, in His Spirit through the language of the Holy Spirit. Scripture says, *"But the hour is coming and now is, when the true worshipers will worship the Father in the spirit and truth; for the Father is seeking such to worship Him."* (John 4:23) Since satan doesn't know the language of heaven (language of the Holy Spirit) anymore, as such, he couldn't

84

understand instructions given to Adam and his wife. Since he was kicked out of heaven, all his privileges were taken away from him, including the Holy Spirit language of truth and holiness. He was filled with evil, which is the spirit of deception and lies. That is why he disguised himself and went to the woman to get more clarity on what God told them, in the garden. Ask God to speak through you with the language of the Holy Spirit. It's available to everyone who believes and has accepted His Son, as Lord of their lives.

> *However, when He, the Spirit of truth, has come, He will guide you into all truth; for He will not speak on His own authority, but whatever He hears He will speak; and He will tell you things to come. He will glorify Me, for He will take of what is Mine and declare it to you. All things that the Father has are Mine. Therefore I said that He will take of Mine and declare it to you. (John 16:13-15)*

> *And for me, that utterance may be given to me, that I may open my mouth boldly to make known the mystery of the gospel for which I am an ambassador in chains; that in it I may speak boldly as I ought to speak. (Ephesians 5:19-20)*

> *Also the Scripture advices us "But you, beloved, building yourselves up on your most holy faith, praying in the Holy Spirit". (Jude 1:20)*

Satan introduced evil and his spirit used the language of deceit and lies to communicate to the rest of humanity. Remember God created Adam and Eve in His Spirit, therefore, they carried the holiness and purity of God, until they were deceived by satan. He always makes man to focus on themselves rather than their Creator. *Then the serpent said to the woman, "You will not surely die. For God knows that in the day you eat of it your eyes will be opened, and you will be like God, knowing good and evil."* (Genesis 3:4-5) He made them doubt God, and shift their focus on themselves, rather than their Creator.

> *You are of your father the devil, and the desires of your father you want to do. He was a murderer from the beginning, and does not stand in the truth, because there is no truth in him. When he speaks a lie, he speaks from his own resources, for he is a liar and the father of it. (John 8:44)*

This initiated the human aspiration to build the tower of Babel, causing the Lord to come down from heaven and confuse their language of deceit and lies. Their entire focus was on themselves and what they can do without their Creator. God confused and scattered them all over the earth, making them speak different languages.

> *"Now the whole earth had one language and one speech. And it came to pass, as they journeyed from the east, that they found a plain in the land of Shinar, and they dwelt there. Then they said*

to one another, come, let us make bricks and bake them thoroughly." They had brick for stone, and they had asphalt for mortar. And they said, Come, let us build ourselves a city, and a tower whose top is in the heavens; let us make a name for ourselves, lest we be scattered abroad over the face of the whole earth." (Genesis 11:1-4)

But the LORD came down to see the city and the tower which the sons of men had built. And the LORD said, "Indeed the people are one and they all have one language, and this is what they begin to do; now nothing that they purpose to do will be withheld from them. Come, let Us go down and there confuse their language, that they may not understand one another's speech." So the LORD scattered them abroad, from there over the face of all the earth, and they ceased building the city. Therefore its name is called Babel, because there the LORD confused the language of all the earth; and from there the LORD scattered them abroad over the face of the earth. (Genesis 11:5-9)

The language of the Holy Spirit is available to all who believe in the Lord Jesus Christ, to communicate to God, through the word of God. The word of God is spirit and life and this language is available for those who believe in His Son. One reason why Christ came was to restore the children of God their original heavenly language, which we lost when man disobeyed God, in the garden. Jesus Christ promised once He goes back to His Father, He will send the Holy Spirit to them on earth. (John 16:13-14)

He will be their Comforter and declare to them all about Jesus. Jesus Christ went to His Father and He sent us the Holy Spirit, according to Acts 2:1-4.

> *Then there appeared to them divided tongues, as of fire, and one sat upon each of them. (Acts 2:3)*

> *And they were all filled with the Holy Spirit and began to speak with other tongues, as the Spirit gave them utterance. (Acts 2:4)*

When satan speaks, he speak from his language of deceit and lies. When God speaks, He speaks from His language of the Holy Spirit: the truth and holiness. Which language are you speaking?

THE WOMAN'S DIALOGUE
WITH THE SERPENT

But each one is tempted when he is drawn away by his own
desires and enticed. Then when desire has conceived, it
gives birth to sin; and sin, when it is full-grown,
brings forth death. (James 1:14-15)

S atan took the form of and became the serpent. Satan in the form of a serpent was waiting for Eve, in the garden. To this day, satan has been roaming around after the children of God, since he was cast out of heaven, in all manner of shapes and forms.

Whenever one talks to the serpent, certain things occur between themselves and the stranger. At any point in the conversation with satan, you can expect one of the following to happen; you may leave from your meeting place and be troubled, or not. You may leave with the stranger, going where satan had initially planned to take you. It all depends on the information the stranger was able to gather from you. Often, that's why, some may leave a person and still hear the voice of that person talking to them, either negative or positive. These voices continue to ring in so many hearts today and they never depart. The voice could have started speaking a long time ago, during childhood. Some are still tormented by those voices. What are you hearing and from whom?

> *So when the woman saw that the tree was good for food, that it was pleasant to the eyes, and a tree desirable to make one wise, she took of its fruit and ate. She also gave to her husband with her, and he ate. Then the eyes of both of them were opened, and they knew that they were naked; and they sewed fig leaves together and made themselves coverings. (Genesis 3:6-7)*

In the case of Eve, when the serpent was talking to her, there was invisible water or food that cannot be seen with the naked eye. It flowed from the serpent, to the woman. This invisible food is delicate to the body. Remember, words are like food, either negative or positive. Words can cause damage to the body and soul, or nourish them. It all depends what kind of food or information you are eating. When you receive negative words, all that flows outward out will be negative. Inversely, if you receive positive words, all that flows out will be positive. Therefore, soak yourself with the Word of God.

> *In the meantime His disciples urged Him, saying, "Rabbi, eat." But He said to them, "I have food to eat of which you do not know." Therefore*

the disciples said to one another, "Has anyone brought Him anything to eat?" Jesus said to them, "My food is to do the will of Him who sent Me, and to finish His work. (John 4:31-34)

I am the living bread which came down from heaven. If anyone eats of this bread, he will live forever; and the bread that I shall give is My flesh, which I shall give for the life of the world. (John 6:51)

The LORD changed satan's appearance from what he used to look like before he corrupted humanity. Therefore, we cannot assume that satan hasn't changed or modified his schemes, as he's still talking, seducing, enticing and deceiving humanity. He's constantly changing his strategy and we can see his numerous appearances in our churches, communities and government offices, for example. He's established vast communication methods to attract people to listen to him in order to gather more souls to his kingdom; whether through people, television, radio, internet, books, videos, etc. Many policies and church doctrines are now far removed from scripture and the original purpose of why Christ came for us.

Once Adam named the animals after they were created, I do not recall in scripture when Adam went back to rename the animals, except when God cursed the serpent. So, God chose to curse the serpent to crawl on the ground and eat dust forever.

"Because you have done this, You are cursed more than all cattle, and more than every beast of

the field; On your belly you shall go, and you shall
eat dust. All the days of your life." (Genesis 3:14)

Why Did God allow satan to enter the Garden?

God allowed satan into the garden knowing he would
tempt Eve and that they would both sin. He told them which
tree to eat from. The decision was about who they would
decide to listen to, God or satan. Why did God do that? Some
people may ask if God will put a murderer and child molester
together in a room with a child, knowing what could happen
to the child. Now, let us look into why God allowed satan in
the garden with His children, even though God knew what
would happen. To blame God would be wrong because God
is God. Here's why.

Adam and Eve were Already in Adulthood

Adam was not a child and neither was his wife. They were
adults, man and woman. He had some knowledge of right and
wrong, because God had told he and his wife not to eat of the
tree of the knowledge of good and evil. In other words, Adam
had been given a commandment to follow; that included the
option to obey or disobey his Creator. The choice was laid out
for them. The issue was about the decision they would make
after given proper instructions, especially from God. Adam and
Eve were made in God's image, but they made an important
moral choice, which was detrimental to their lives. Who are
you talking to?

Adam and Eve knew about the good and evil

We could argue further, is it okay to put a grown man in a room with a murderer? Why not, as long this man is capable and strong, both physically and spiritually. Most of us have been in rooms with murderers and assassins on numerous occasions, and had no idea such a person was around us, while going to the mall, hospital, church, and so on. All that happened in the garden between satan and Eve, was a crafty discussion going on, during which the serpent deceived the woman. So was it wrong to put a murderer in a room with a man, if the only thing that could happen was that they were going to have a conversation? There is nothing wrong with that, even when you know the bad person is cleverer than you. Always remember that those in Christ are the good ones and bad cannot ever override the good. It is impossible for the darkness to overtake the Light.

> *In Him was life and the life was the light of men. And the light shines in the darkness, and the darkness did not comprehend it. (John 1:4-5)*

According to scripture, the good person chooses to remain good.

> *The Holy Spirit convicts us with the righteousness of God. And when He has come, He will convict the world of sin and of righteousness, and of judgment: of sin, because they do not believe in Me; of righteousness, because I go to My Father and*

you see Me no more; of judgment, because the
ruler of this world is judged. (John 16: 8-11)

The righteous person knows what the right choice is sup-
posed to be. Therefore, he is not defenseless or helpless. God
does no wrong and he has his reasons for allowing people to
be tempted. Scripture even tells us that Jesus was led into the
wilderness by the Holy Spirit, to be tempted. (Matthew 4:1-3)
The LORD God wants to know, if we will abide in His law, that
is, His commandments.

Did God cause Adam and Eve to sin?

The same principle that God offered to the angels when He
created them, was applied to mankind, which is free will. Eve
wasn't there when angels and the serpent were created, so she
didn't know the craftiness of the serpent. Eve freely chose to
listen to the serpent when presented with the fruit and to rebel
against God. Adam fell because he freely chose to disobey
God, while listening to his wife, who had also chosen to disobey. It was a choice both made in full knowledge of what was
right and wrong. The LORD told them when they were placed
in the Garden of Eden, not to eat from the tree of knowledge
of good and evil.

God warned Adam and Eve because He created the Serpent

God gave them freedom to choose. Freedom, however,
has the propensity to cause temptation. Therefore, freedom of

choice means that temptations will occur. Conversely, if there is no free will, there is no temptation.

Adam and Eve were made in the image of God and given free will, which gave the option of rebellion, an option that was provided by the devil. Satan transgressed against God as satan's ultimate goal is to recruit men and women to his dark world. The devil is here, on earth, and that's why Jesus came. It requires Jesus Christ's sinless blood, for us to boldly confront the enemy of God. Jesus Christ came to give us the Holy Spirit and through the Word of God, we should know which tree we should be eating from, as Jesus is the bread of life and the tree of life.

> *And Jesus said to them, "I am the bread of life. He who comes to Me shall never hunger, and he who believes in Me shall never thirst. (John 6:35)*

> *I am the living bread which came down from heaven. If anyone eats of this bread, he will live forever; and the bread that I shall give is My flesh, which I shall give for the life of the world. (John 6:51)*

> *Then the Lord God said, "Behold, the man has become like one of Us, to know good and evil. And now, lest he put out his hand and take also of the tree of life, and eat, and live forever" (Genesis 3:22)*

So He drove out the man; and He placed cher-
ubim at the east of the garden of Eden, and a
flaming sword which turned every way, to guard
the way to the tree of life. (Genesis 3:24)

"He who has an ear, let him hear what the Spirit
says to the churches. To him who overcomes I
will give to eat from the tree of life, which is in the
midst of the Paradise of God."' (Revelation 2:7)

In the middle of its street, and on either side of
the river, was the tree of life, which bore twelve
fruits, each tree yielding its fruit every month.
The leaves of the tree were for the healing of the
nations. (Revelation 22:2)

Finally, why did God let Satan into the garden knowing what
would happen? It was His will to do so. The Lord gave free will
to angels in heaven and also gave it to mankind, when they
were created. We all have choices to make, of good or evil.
It all depends who we're listening to, in order to make such
choices. His children must respond to His instruction and be
obedient to His commandments, in this beautiful garden, He
created for us.

Let no one say when he is tempted, "I am tempted
by God"; for God cannot be tempted by evil, nor
does He Himself tempt anyone. But each one
is tempted when he is drawn away by his own
desires and enticed. Then, when desire has

conceived, it gives birth to sin; and sin, when it is full-grown, brings forth death. (James 1:13-15)

There are questions we must ask ourselves.

Who are you talking to? Are you still listening to the serpent? Are you obeying the instructions of God that He has given you? There are eight critical questions, for those in the Kingdom of God must ask themselves, in any given situation.

1. What did you hear first from God?
2. Whose voice are you hearing now?
3. What are you looking at?
4. Where are you focusing your attention?
5. What kind of dialogue are you engaging in?
6. From where are you seeking your information?
7. From where are you seeking your knowledge?
8. What benefits are motivating your decisions?

Tree of Mixed Fruit.

Here's an analogy. If you pour clean water inside a glass, you see through the glass and through the water. However, when you pour colored water or liquid inside a glass you cannot see through with same clarity, as with clean water. Let's assume the clear water in the glass represents good, while the colored liquid represents evil.

If you mixed the clear water (good) and colored liquid (evil) together you will notice it has changed to a colored liquid. If you choose to drink whatever's in the glass, you are drinking both the good and evil at the same time. How? Drinking from this mixture, you have drunk both the water representing good, and the colored liquid, representing evil. It would require quite a vigorous purification process to bring clarity back to this mixture again. The fruit of the tree of the knowledge of good and evil remains on that tree. If you bite one fruit from this tree, you have eaten both good and evil.

How could this colored mixture liquid in the glass cup be made pure and clear again? It requires the continuous addition of gallons of clear water to the mixture. The additional water also represents the Holy Spirit and the word of God, by which all traces of evil can be washed and purged out completely. The good inside man was tainted by an unclean spirit, just like the liquid mixture in the glass.

Every human has good and evil in us since our first parents obeyed satan. Now it requires that we pour more water, representing the Holy Spirit and the word of God in our lives. We need to continually feed on the word of God to perfect us, until the day of Jesus Christ. Jesus Christ the living Word, came so that we can have life more abundantly. (John 1:1, 10:10) Our relationship with Christ requires effort from us also. If we say we have faith or believe in Him, we must demonstrate it through our constant fellowship with him. Therefore, let us continuously flush our spirit beings, with His word; nor allow traces of evil to take root in us, by engaging ourselves in the word of God.

CHAPTER SIX

A WOMAN'S DIALOGUE WITH JESUS

Must always think well of God as the Good Father. Do not call anyone on earth your Father; for One is your Father, He who is in heaven (Matthew 23:9)

Several women had dialogues with Jesus and the result was always unique, transparent, prosperous and eternally successful. Jesus came to share the Kingdom of His Father in heaven, with the children of God on earth. His goal was to change the destructive and sinful, human mind and heart, which all started when the enemy came to interrogate the first woman in the garden. Jesus Christ came to renew our minds and cleanse us from sin, bringing us back to His Father's Kingdom. Women, such as Mary, Martha and others, weren't all that different from the story of the Samaritan woman, which we'll discuss.

There is something spectacular to applaud about this Samaritan woman, who encountered Jesus. The Samaritan woman doesn't appear, nor is discussed anywhere else in the bible, however, centuries later, spiritual leaders and theologians continue to analyze and share her encounter with Jesus. Her unique appointment with Jesus also compelled me to add her story as well.

Whomever you talk to in life, the word you receive from that person could bring death or life. Choose well before you engage in any conversation. As mentioned before, if you left a conversation saddened, tormented, in despair, down, frustrated, or unmotivated, it's possible you just finished talking to enemy of God, and its result is deadly. On the other hand, if you've left a dialogue and are happy, joyful, upbeat, bubbly, motivated, spiritually inspired, optimistic and your heart swells with joy, you probably just received a word from the Lord, and the result is eternal blessing. Who is talking to you? And, who you are listening to is important. Let's explore Jesus' conversation with the Samaritan woman.

The Samaritan woman was thirsty and she needed to get water. She decided to go and fetch water as usual from Jacob's well, which Jacob gave to his son Joseph. This time was quite different, as Jesus was waiting for her at the well that day. What she will realize is her need for the living water, which only comes from Christ, the Messiah.

Samaritan Woman Found an Ocean Instead of a Well

Christ, the Anointed One, knew the Samaritan woman was spiritually thirsty, requiring the fountain of living waters from Him, to quench all her thirsts. Since Jesus knows all our needs, he knew the needs of this woman.

The woman was probably thirsty for many things: relationship, family, fellowship, peace, joy, etc. In addition, she may have also suffered reproach and feelings of inferiority. After all, she had five husbands previously and the man she was with, at that time, wasn't her husband. I imagine Jesus has heard her crying behind the closed doors. He has heard her from afar and in her darkest moments and now he's come to her where and when she's least expected it. Many times our life situations look hauntingly similar to this woman's life.

Jews normally don't normally travel on a Samaritan road, but Jesus chose to travel this road at the time anyway. Jesus started to talk to her and asked her for water to drink. Jesus being sociable and loves to speak with those who are thirsty for Him, yet don't know it yet and He knows what we lack. This was a divine connection for the woman.

As she approached the well, the woman identified Jesus as a Jew but didn't know Him as Jesus, the Messiah. She thought He was just another Jew demanding something from a Samaritan. She replied *"For Jews have no dealing with Samaritans."* (John 4:9c) What she didn't realize was that Jesus came to have a relationship with all people.

Jesus came to give us eternal life. The Samaritan woman received eternal life the day she encountered Jesus. We should know then, Jesus can meet us anywhere, as He is ready to meet us at any point of our lives. Don't doubt Him.

> *Jesus answered and said to her, "If you knew the gift of God, and who it is who says to you, 'Give Me a drink,' you would have asked Him, and He would have given you living water." (John 4:10)*

As we've discussed before, when exchanging words or dialogue with someone, you are actually eating or drinking from them. How? Words are invisible food or water, whether intentional or not. According to one parable of Jesus, in the book of Luke, a seed is the word of God.

> *"Now the parable is this: The seed is the word of God." (Luke 8:11)*

It is clear that a seed can be eaten, so also spiritually, the word of God can be eaten. Any time you are engaging in any form of dialogue with someone, understand you are actually eating or drinking, through exchanging words. What kind of word are you receiving? Whoever is talking to you does matter and what a person is saying to you is important to notice.

The word of God is Spirit and life. The disciples came to Jesus, asking whether He'd eaten that day.

> *In the meantime His disciples urged Him, saying, "Rabbi, eat."* ***But He said to them, "I have food to eat of which you do not know."*** *Therefore the disciples said to one another, "Has anyone brought Him anything to eat?" Jesus said to them, "My food is to do the will of Him who sent Me and to finish His work. (John 4:31-34)*

Jesus is the Word and when we speak the word of God to people, we are planting seeds. Jesus is the living water who can quench every thirst. Jesus began to address the problem of this woman from the root, although the woman did not know this at beginning of their dialogue. The Samaritan woman met Jesus while conducting a mundane task, at the well, and His word filled her completely, with absolute joy.

> *Jesus answered and said to her, Whoever drinks of this water will thirst again, but whoever drinks of the water that I will give him will never thirst, But the water that I shall give him will become in him a fountain of water springing up into everlasting life. (John 4:14)*

Suddenly, something changed within her, this woman awakened in the spirit, and she quickly replied to Jesus. *"Sir, give me this water that I may not thirst, nor come here to draw."* (John 4:15) Since this Samaritan woman was born, she's probably gone through numerous challenges in life, especially numerous unstable and broken relationships. Her life seemed to consist of going from one man to another.

Jesus said to her, "Go, call your husband and come here." (John 4:16) He knew she never had good steady relationship. Jesus confronted her with the darkest part of her life. We must confess our sins and that was the perfect opportunity Jesus used to allow the Samaritan to confess hers. Jesus knows all our challenges.

The Samaritan woman at the well was not perfect, nor was she trying to be. She was impressed that Jesus knew all her sins. (John 4:18) Jesus is also the only one who can forgive sins. As a result, she believed the Messiah, the Anointed One. At a certain point of their conversation, the woman replied to Jesus,

*The woman said to Him, "Sir, give me this water,
that I may not thirst, nor come here again.
(John 4:15)*

When you stay long enough in the presence of Almighty,
you will get to know Jesus better than ever before. Something
great will always come at the end of it, which is eternal life.
Jesus did not come to condemn but to give us eternal life,
regardless of any sins we have committed. (John 3:17) This
woman received eternal life, went back to the city and brought
both men and women to Jesus.

Jesus came for her and all the Samaritans.

Jesus explained to the woman at the well that God is Spirit,
and those who worship Him must worship him in spirit and in
truth. This woman came to realize she had been talking with
Jesus, the Messiah. An inferior, poor Samaritan woman, with
many issues, met the Jewish Jesus Christ, in an unexpected
place. So yes, Jesus came for everyone. The Samaritan experienced a renewed Spirit.

One Encounter with Jesus Changed her life

The Samaritan woman's encounter with Jesus changed her
life forever. Scripture illustrates how she became an evangelist
to the nation of Samaria. She went back to the city without her
bucket of water and brought others to Jesus. They all believed
her and they also believed Jesus when they met Him. Jesus

stayed with them a couple extra days, because of His word and many more Samaritans became believers.

The purpose of Jesus Christ death, burial and resurrection on the third day, is to spread the Gospel to everyone and to all nations. Jesus only needs one person from one family or nation. He will make sure those people will go back to share the Good News, with those who don't know Him, just like the Samaritan woman did. She met Jesus and went back to her city to tell others about Christ.

> *The woman left her water bucket, went her way into the city and said to the men, Come, see a Man who told me all things that I ever did, Could this be the Christ? They came out of the city and came to Him. (John 4:28-30)*

The Samaritan woman's life and the people around her were changed forever. She went to the city and told the Samaritans all about Jesus whom she just met. She had one encounter with Jesus and the power of the Anointed One rested upon her forever. She went to confess all around the city, that surely Jesus is Lord. It is impossible to meet Jesus, the Anointed One, and not know the truth. He is the truth and the Word. As a result, this woman did not have anymore secrets, as she relayed the secrets of her life. Now she's no longer ashamed of her past, because of her encounter with the Anointed One. She was boldly talking about Jesus to everyone she met!

> *And many of the Samaritan of that city believed in Him because of the word of the woman who*

testified, He told me all that I ever did." So when the Samaritans had come to Him, they urged Him to stay with them; and He stayed there two days. And many more believed because of His own word. (John 4:39-41)

All this happened because a Samaritan woman went out to fetch water one afternoon from a well and the Lord ordered her steps. Her sins were washed away completely by Jesus. Her story demonstrates how Jesus offers divine mercy, in the living water of grace, washing away all sins and cleansing our souls. The woman went to the well to get a bucket of water and instead, she got the proverbial ocean.

Disparity of the two Women at the well and the garden

This woman's story teaches us that God finds us worthy of His love in spite of our bankrupt lives. Jesus actually valued this woman and every one of us, to have intimacy with Him. Only a person like the Samaritan woman, an outcast from her own people, could understand what it means to be wanted and cared for, when no one else cared.

He met a woman at the well and ministered to all the Samaritan people. This demonstrates to us, that Jesus only needs a few of us who desire Him to bring salvation to all nations.

The dialogue of Jesus at the well, with the Samaritan woman and the dialogue of the serpent in the garden were dramatically different. The first woman was enticed and deceived by the serpent. Therefore Satan caused man to disobey God and forced man from their God-given dominion. The woman of Samaria and other Samaritans met Jesus and their lives changed forever, for the better. Who you are talking to matters, it will determine your destiny from here on the earth, to eternity.

CHAPTER SEVEN

OTHER WOMEN IMPEACHED

They too were not at the naming ceremony. Satan beguiled the first woman to deceive humanity from its rightful position of dominion on earth.

I mpeachment is the act of bringing an accusation or charge against someone, group or community, either publicly or privately. This has happened in every generation since God created the first man and woman that walked on earth. There may be degrees of impeachment or accusation, but they all come from the same source, the devil. The accuser of the brethren is the god of this world; cast out from heaven, due to disobedience and rebellion. Satan continues to wage war from all directions, against God and His children. Eve, however, set the precedent of impeachment from satan, for all women, whom God made in His own image.

But their minds were blinded. For until this day the same veil remains unlifted in the reading of the Old Testament, because the veil is taken away in Christ. (2 Corinthians 3:14)

Whose minds the god of this age has blinded, who do not believe, lest the light of the gospel of the glory of Christ, who is the image of God, should shine on them. (2 Corinthians 4:4)

And Adam was not deceived, but the woman being deceived, fell into transgression. (1 Timothy 2:14)

Now the serpent was more cunning than any beast of the field which the LORD God had made. And he said to the woman "Has God indeed said, You shall not eat of every tree of the garden? (Genesis 3:1)

Since then, women continue to receive accusations and allegations from both men and women, about what happened in the garden. However, when God saw the situation of Adam and his wife in the garden, He went straight to Adam to inquire why they disobeyed Him. Adam replied to the LORD God, and said it was the woman that you gave me, she gave me of the tree and I ate. The LORD then went to the nameless woman, Adam's wife, and she replied that satan deceived her.

Then the man said. "The woman who You gave to be with me, she gave me of the tree, and I ate."

110

And the LORD God said to the woman, "What is this you have done?" The woman said, "The serpent deceived me, and I ate." (Genesis 3:12, 13)

Yet whenever we discover something that a woman or women have done, if you take a closer look, you will always find a man behind it. Men unfortunately always turn around to say "She did it." If Satan did not do it, the natural man will cause it to happen. If Adam had been walking closely with his wife in the garden, he could have saved his wife from the evil interrogation, caused by the serpent. This impeachment will continue until men know their position and understand their responsibilities to protect women, from the whiles of satan. Men and women should examine closely what information they're bringing home. Remember, the information you receive is like invisible food or water.

Other women in the Bible who were also impeached, are listed here and you will find that men were always the originators of the deceit. These women listed here were all impeached, either by a man or a woman. Let's take a look at each of the following accounts of how satan got them impeached. Remember, if satan can get you to change the way you think about something, he can get you to do it another way, which is not of God. His goal is to attack the children of God through their thinking, hearts, minds, emotions and conscience.

Sarah Impeached (Abraham's wife)

Sarah, Abraham's wife, was advanced in age and did not have a child until her old age. God had promised Abraham that he will be the father of all nations. (Genesis12:2, 3) Since both Abraham and Sarah were advanced in age, Sarah decided to help God achieved His plan. Sarah motivated and inspired her husband, Abraham, to lie with her Egyptian maidservant, Hagar, so that they could have the son that was promised. Hagar conceived and had a son called Ishmael. Now we have two lineages coming from Abraham, Ishmael and Isaac.

Sarah impeached Hagar and her husband even though she suggested Hagar be with her husband, initially. Sarah, Abraham and Hagar were all impeached or accused together because the same serpent convinced Sarah to eat from wrong tree. (Genesis 12:2-3; 16:1-16; 17:1-8)

Hagar Impeached (Sarah's Maidservant)

The Egyptian maidservant had no choice but to obey her master, Sarah. Sarah told Hagar to go in with her husband, because she could not have a child on her own. The Egyptian woman did as her master has commanded her, and she was the first woman to have a child with Abraham. This altered the promise that God had planned for Abraham. Hagar was kicked out of their tent to find a place for her and her child. Hagar was impeached as a result of her master. (Genesis 16:11-16)

Rebekah Impeached (Isaac's wife)

Rebekah conceived and was carrying twins in her womb, but these babies were struggling inside her, so she consulted with God about them. The LORD told Rebekah the older child, shall serve the younger. This was the first time recorded in scripture, that a woman asked God something directly when she was not clear about something. Rebekah gave birth to Esau and Jacob. These children grew older and their father also advanced in age. His eyes were dim, but he called his older son, Esau to bless him before he died. Rebekah over-heard Isaac's plan, which completely contradicted God's plan that she received while she was carrying them in her womb. When Rebekah heard Isaac's plan towards Esau, the spirit of the LORD arose within her and she remembered well all what she had received from God.

> *"Two nations inside are in your womb, two peo-ples shall be separated from your body; One people shall be stronger than the other, And the older shall serve the younger." (Genesis 25:23)*

Therefore, she partnered with God so Jacob could be blessed instead of Esau, as God originally planned. She was impeached then, and till today many people believe that Rebekah loved one child more than the other. Man will often impeach you when you are obeying your Creator. Remember, whatever the LORD has told you that you are here to fulfill those tasks successfully. (Genesis 25:19-34)

Rachel Impeached (Jacob's wife)

Jacob was married to the two daughters of Laban. The elder was Leah and the younger was named Rachel. It was tra-dition at that time for the older daughter to get married before the younger.

113

> *Leah's eyes were delicate, but Rachel was beau-*
> *tiful of form and appearance. (Genesis 29:10)*

Jacob loved Rachel. He told Laban that he will serve him seven years so that he can marry Rachel. He didn't love Leah, however, Laban tricked Jacob into marrying her. Leah conceived and had Reuben as the first son to Jacob, while Rachel was barren. Leah conceived again and had Simeon, Levi, Judah, Issachar, Dinah etc. When the Lord remembered Rachel, God listened to her and opened her womb and she bore a child named Joseph. (Genesis 30:22-24).

While about to leave for Bethel, as God had commanded, Jacob instructed his household to put away foreign idols. Unfortunately, his wife Rachel had taken one of her father's household idols with her, when they left.

> *And Jacob said to his household and to all who*
> *were with him, Put away the foreign gods that*
> *are among you, purify yourselves, and change*
> *your garments. (Genesis 35:2)*

Laban came after Jacob, when he was looking for his household idols and, Jacob said to Laban, whoever, stole your idols shall die, as Jacob didn't know his wife, Rachel, had taken them.

With whomever you find your gods, do not let him live. In the presence of our brethren, identify what I have of yours and take it with you." For Jacob did not know that Rachel had stolen them. *(Genesis 31:32, 33)*

Now Rachel had taken the household idols, put them in the camel saddle and sat on them. And Laban searched all about the tent but did not find them. (Genesis 31:34)

And she said to her father, "Let it not displease my lord that I cannot rise before you, for the manner of women is with me." And he searched but did not find the household idols. (Genesis 31:35)

Later, Rachel died on the journey to Bethel and was buried at Ephrath, also called Bethlehem, at the childbirth of her son Benjamin.

Then they journeyed from Bethel. And when there was but a little distance to go to Ephrath, Rachel labored in childbirth, and she had hard labor. Now it came to pass, when she was in hard labor, that the midwife said to her, "Do not fear; you will have this son also." And so it was, as her soul was departing (for she died), that she called his name Ben-Oni; but his father called him Benjamin. So Rachel died and was buried on the way to Ephrath (that is, Bethlehem). And Jacob set a pillar on her grave, which is the pillar of Rachel's grave to this day. (Genesis 35:16-20)

Bathsheba Impeached (David's request for Uriah's wife)

Bathsheba, the wife of Uriah, was at home taking a bath when King David saw her beauty from his palace and asked for her. David sent a messenger to invite her and she came and David laid with her. (2 Samuel 11:2) Then he sent her home where she later discovered that she had conceived David's child. She came back and told David that she had conceived. David plotted to have her husband killed at the war front. After she heard that her husband had been killed, she mourned for him. David sent for her and married her and she bore him a son. David had displeased the LORD. (2 Samuel 11:27) David was the one who orchestrated the schemes toward Uriah and Bathsheba. However, we can also surmise that many have impeached Bathsheba, concerning the relationship she developed with King David.

Tamar Impeached (David's Daughter)

David's son Absolom, had a sister called Tamar. *Amnon was so distressed in love for his sister Tamar, that he became sick; for she was a virgin. And it was improper for Amnon to do anything to her.* (2 Samuel 13:2). Jonadab helped Amnon in a scheme to attack his own sister. So Amnon pretended he was sick and David sent his daughter Tamar to Amnon's house to cook for him. While Amnon was in his bedroom, he asked Tamar to bring the food, she had prepared for him to the bedroom so that he can eat from her hand. Of course, Tamar wasn't aware of the plot, which her brother Amnon and his friend Jonadab had planned against her. Therefore,

116

she took the food to his brother in his bedroom as he has requested.

> *Now when she had brought them to him to eat, he took hold of her and said to her, Come, lie with me, my sister." But she answered him, "No, my brother, do not force me, for no such thing should be done in Israel. Do not do this disgraceful thing!" (2 Samuel 13:12-13)*

I believe it was probably one the consequences of David's sin. The evil started when David took Uriah's wife for himself while her husband was at war. David daughter; Tamar was impeached by her brother, and his friend Jonadab. Her only crime was to care for her own brother and he raped her.

Solomon's foreign wives and Queen of Sheba Impeached
(foreign wives and Sheba)

After David died, Solomon was enthroned. God blessed Solomon and he built an incredible temple for God. The queen of Sheba heard about the fame of Solomon, concerning the name of the LORD, so she came to Solomon to test him with hard questions. This queen indeed believed in Solomon and after she had seen all that he had built. Then she said to the king: "It was a true report which I heard in my own land about your words and your wisdom. However I did not believe the words until I came and saw with my own eyes; and indeed the half was not told me. Your wisdom and prosperity exceed the fame of which I heard. (1Kings 10:6-7) She came with precious gold, spices and precious stones in great quantity. (1King 10:10-11) She gave so much and there was never again such an abundance of spices as the queen of Sheba gave to King Solomon. Before returning to her country, Solomon was pleased with her and he gave her much in return.

> *King Solomon gave to the queen of Sheba all she desired, whatever she asked, much more than she had brought to the king. So she turned and went to her country, she and her servants. (2 Chronicle 9:12)*

When the queen of Sheba came to visit Solomon, she brought him precious gifts. (2 Chronicles 9:13) This calls to question, did she bring idols with her from her own country to Solomon's palace? As carrying idols while traveling was customary at that time. If so, did Solomon allow those idols into the palace or God's holy temple? Later, Sheba's statement to Solomon recognized the mighty God that Solomon worshiped, by the wisdom he displayed when she met with him. It was clear that Solomon's God was quite different from her gods.

> *Blessed be the Lord your God, who delighted in you, setting you on His throne to be king for the Lord **your** God! Because your God has loved Israel, to establish them forever, therefore He made you king over them, to do justice and righteousness." (2 Chronicles 9:8)*

After a while, when the queen of Sheba had gone back to her country, King Solomon loved many foreign women as well as Pharaoh's daughter he married, women of Moabites, Ammonites, Edomites, Sidonians and Hittites. (1 Kings 11:1) "For it was so, when Solomon was old, that his wives turned his heart after other gods; and his heart was not loyal to the LORD his God, as was the heart of his father David." (1 Kings 11:4) His wives erected and displayed their idols and gods in the holy temple, which Solomon had built for God.

For Solomon went after Ashtoreth the goddess of the Sidonians, and after Milcom the abomination of the Ammonites. (1 Kings 11:5)

> *Solomon did evil in the sight of the LORD, and did not fully follow the LORD, as did his father David. (1 Kings 11:6)*

> *Then Solomon built a high place for Chemosh the abomination of Moab, on the hill that is east of Jerusalem, and for Molech the abomination of the people of Ammon. (1 Kings 11:7)*

The LORD was not pleased with Solomon. As the scripture says, you cannot serve two masters. The Lord blessed Solomon before these women came on the scene: queen of Sheba and his foreign wives, from among the Moabites, Ammonites, Edomites, Sidonians and Hittites. They came and corrupted all that God had done through the hands of Solomon. If Solomon had refused to allow idols in the palace, nor associated with or married foreign women, which God had warned him before; Solomon's foreign wives wouldn't have been impeached for the fall of the kingdom and quite possibly, the queen of Sheba either.

Delilah Impeached (Samson's wife)

Samson was mighty among his people and he had fought lions and Philistines ruthlessly. Now it came to pass, when Samson's moral weakness grew and expanded, he went to Gaza to meet a harlot. (Judges 16:1-2)

> *Then Samson said: "With the jawbone of a donkey, Heaps upon heaps, with the jawbone of a donkey I have slain a thousand men!" (Judges 15:16)*

Later, it came to pass, Samson loved a woman from the valley of Sorek, whose name was Delilah. Unfortunately, he fell in-love with a woman who loves money more than him. Delilah was coerced by the Philistines to learn the source of Samson's great strength. She was promised eleven hundred pieces of silver, if she could find where his strength lies.

> *And the lords of the Philistines came up to her and said to her, Entice him, and find out where his great strength lies, and by what means we may overpower him, that we may bind him to afflict him; and every one of us will give you eleven hundred pieces of silver." (Judges 16:5)*

Delilah induced her husband to share the secret of his power and strength.

> *So Delilah said to Samson, Please tell me where your great strength lies, and with what you may be bound to afflict you. And Samson said to her, "If they bind me with seven fresh bowstrings, not yet dried, then I shall become weak, and be like any other man." (Judges 16:7)*

> *So he said to her, "If they bind me securely with new ropes that have never been used, then I shall become weak, and be like any other man"." (Judges 16:11)*

> *And he said to her, if you weave the seven locks of my head into the web of the loom" (Judges 16:13)*

Samson was tormented day and night by Delilah to reveal the secret of his strength.

> *Then she said to him, "How can you say, I love you, when your heart is not with me? You have mocked me these tree times, and have not told me where your great strength lies." (Judges 16:15)*

And as she continued to pester him daily, her words pressed him until his soul was vexed. Delilah was persistent as she had her eyes focused on the benefit she will gain from this transaction with the Philistines. She didn't care about her husband's position.

> *That he told her all his heart, and said to her, "No razor has ever come upon my head, for I have been a Nazirite to God from my mother's womb. If I am shaven, then my strength will leave me, and I shall become weak, and be like any other man." (Judges 16:17)*

Delilah loved money, so she pursued her husband to the point of death. She was willing to prostitute herself to capture her husband, because of the great monetary benefit she'd gain out of the deal. Delilah was enticed with the highest compensation ever, from her husband's enemy, the Philistines. Delilah pursued, enticed, induced and tormented her husband to the point of death, because of her motivation for money and she was impeached.

Lot's Wife Impeached

The name of Lot's wife was not mentioned in the Bible and even when Christ referenced her in scripture, her name was not disclosed. God sent angels of the LORD to remove Lot and his family, from the land of Sodom and Gomorrah. When they left this corruptible city, the only person that looked back was Lot's wife. We could speculate that while she looked back, it was probably because she missed what she had experienced in the land. Her two daughters did not look back, but she did and turned into a pillar of salt. Her impeachment was the fact that she looked back at which the LORD has sent His angels to remove them from.

> *But his wife looked back behind him, and she became a pillar of salt. (Genesis 19:26)*

> *Remember Lot's wife. (Luke 17:32)*

Lot's Daughters Impeached

Lot left Sodom with his two daughters and went to live in a cave. After awhile, these two women had been in a cave with their father alone, and didn't know any other men. Therefore, Lot's two daughters planned to get their father drunk, so they can each lay with him, to have a child. The older daughter went in first and was followed by her younger sister, the next night. These two daughters may have maintained the experiences of Sodom, in their minds. They both conceived and had two sons by their own father. Lot fathered Moab and Ammon through his two daughters. They are the Moabites and Ammonities of today. (Genesis 19:30-38)

Two Women with Sons Impeached (at Solomon's Court)

Two women were brought to Solomon's palace, because one woman's son died while sleeping with his mother. While the other woman slept, the other women switched the dead child with her housemate's living child.

The first woman said, "O my lord, this woman and I dwell in the same house; and I gave birth while she was in the house. Then it happened, the third day after I had given birth, that this woman also gave birth. And we were together; no one was with us in the house, except the two of us in the house. And this woman's son died in the night, because she lay on him. (1 Kings 3:17-19)

Then the other woman said, "No! But the living one is my son, and the dead one is your son." And the first woman said, "No! But the dead one is your son, and the living one is my son." Thus they spoke before the king. (1 Kings 3:22)

The LORD had equipped Solomon with wisdom that had never been seen or experienced before. Solomon judged these two women and asked them to cut the child still living, in half.

Then the woman whose son was living spoke to the king, for she yearned with compassion for her son; and she said, "O my lord, give her the living child, and by no means kill him!" But the other said, "Let him be neither mine nor yours, but divide him." (1Kings 3:26)

Immediately, the woman whose child had died while sleeping, agreed with the king's decision, while the mother of the living child, refused to have the child cut in two and asked the king to give the child alive, to the other woman.

So the king answered and said, "Give the first woman the living child, and by no means kill him; she is his mother. (1 Kings 3:27)

From here, the wisdom of God prevailed and the King knew the son that is alive belong to this woman who refused her son to be caught into two. (1King 3:17-27)

Woman Caught in Adultery Impeached

A woman was caught in adultery and the accusers brought her to Jesus. It was the law of the land that when a woman is caught in adultery, she should be stoned to death. (John 8:3-10)

Then the scribes and Pharisees brought to Him a woman caught in adultery, and when they had set her in the midst, they said to Him, "Teacher, this woman was caught in adultery, in the very act." (John 8:3-4)

This woman was brought to Jesus because she was caught in adultery. Though, she was not committing adultery all by herself, they did not bring the other party to Jesus, they only brought the woman. I believe this may be because she had been with the other men accusing her. Men impeached the woman, but did not impeach the man or men with whom she had committed adultery. The accuser of brethren has always accused women from the beginning of creation, as it remains today. No man was accused along with her, even though we know she wasn't committing adultery by herself.

So when they continued asking Him, He raise Himself up and said to them, "He who is without sin among you, let him throw a stone at her first." (John 8:7)

> *Then those who heard it, being convicted by their conscience, went out one by one, beginning with the oldest even to the last. And Jesus was left alone, and the woman standing in the midst. When Jesus had raised Himself up and saw no one but the woman, He said to her, "Woman, where are those accusers of yours? Has no one condemned you?" (John 8:9, 10)*

CHAPTER EIGHT

JESUS COMMUNICATES WITH HIS CHURCH

*But the time will come when the Bridegroom will be taken
away from them, and then they will fast in those days.
(Matthew 9:15b)*

J esus Christ is coming for His church soon and He's getting us ready for this glorious day. Scripture explains that a church could be a building or group of Christians, in which the followers of Christ gather together to fellowship with one another, in the love of Christ. Yet also the church is the spiritual woman or bride of Christ. Christ not only came to die for our sin and take His bride home with Him, but also to share what He expects from His bride, with love. He came to share His word, as He is the Living Word and our Bridegroom. As husbands to wives, so also Christ is to His church.

Since Jesus departed from earth, there have been miraculous shifts in Christianity, that have led more people to come to know Him and as a result, His church has grown more than any other religion on earth. Christ was born to die for us and His goal while on earth was to reconcile men back to their Creator; and to the kingdom from which they were forced to exit, because of disobedience. Christ came to share the kingdom of heaven with us, yet He also came to share His Father's expectations of His children.

The woman said to Him, "I know that Messiah is coming" (who is called Christ). "When He comes, He will tell us all things." (John 4:25)

Jesus Christ Has Overcome the World

"These things I have spoken to you in figurative language; but the time is coming when I will no longer speak to you in figurative language, but I will tell you plainly about the Father. (John 16:25)

For what is our hope, or joy, or crown of rejoicing? Is it not even you in the presence of our Lord Jesus Christ at His coming? (1 Thessalonians 2:19)

And every spirit that does not confess that Jesus Christ has come in the flesh is not of God. And this is the spirit of the Antichrist, which you have heard was coming, and is now already in the world. (1 John 4:3)

Beware of Antichrist Deceivers

For many deceivers have gone out into the world who do not confess Jesus Christ as coming in the flesh. This is a deceiver and an antichrist. (2 John1:7)

After Jesus has been teaching His disciples for a while, Jesus Christ asked them a revealing question. *"Who do men say that I, the Son of Man, am?* (Matthew16:13b) They begin to tell Him all kind of names, such as John the Baptist, Elijah, Jeremiah and one of the prophets. He asked them again *"But who do you say I am?"* (Matthew 16:15b). *Then Simon Peter, replied to Him and said "You are the Christ, Son of the living God."* Jesus understood that Peter had just caught the revelation from heaven.

"Blessed are you, Simon Bar-Jonah for flesh and blood had not revealed this to you, but My Father who is in heaven. And I also say to you that you are Peter, and on this rock, I will <u>build My Church</u> and the gates of Hades shall not prevail against it." (Matthew 16:17, 18)

Jesus knew this was not a mere mental understanding of Him, but Peter had received revelation from heaven. When He departed from the earth, to His Father in heaven, the church became the central focus of His ministry. Jesus would manage the church from heaven, through the work of the Holy Spirit.

Also Jesus promised and assured us that He will come as a bridegroom to take His bride home.

> *And Jesus said to them, "Can the friends of the bridegroom mourn as long as the bridegroom is with them. But the days will come when the bridegroom will be taken away from them, and then they will fast. (Matthew 9:15)*

Jesus Christ is the Bridegroom and is coming soon for His bride. In parallel, according to scripture, the church will meet the bridegroom, on that glorious day. As husband is to his wife, so also Jesus Christ is to His church. Spiritually, a woman is the symbol of a church and while husband is the symbol of Jesus Christ. In a church congregation, the pastor represents the shepherd, Jesus Christ, our true Shepherd.

> *But I want you to know that the head of every man is Christ, the head of woman is man, and the head of Christ is God. (1Corinthians 11:3)*

Jesus Christ is coming for His church soon. He also said to them that, the gates of Hades shall not prevail against it. I believe churches are asleep at this present age and many things have cropped up within. The word brethren are receiving now are diluted with all sorts of doctrine that are not part of Christ, when he established the church. The old serpent did not stay where he belongs anymore, but is now appearing in churches across the globe, manipulating God's children, from the doctrine of Jesus Christ.

Satan, on the other hand is manifesting himself more boldly than ever; deceiving mankind away from the Kingdom of God, to his kingdom of darkness.

Satan has planted his fallen angels as agents in churches, to continue to administer wrong doctrine to the sons and daughters of Adam and Eve all over again. Jesus Christ came to give us His word, which is truth and life. Satan came to induce and introduce the children of God to false doctrine that comes from him. Here are some examples below.

Destructive Doctrines

> *But there were also false prophets among the people, even as there will be false teachers among you, who will secretly bring in destructive heresies, even denying the Lord who bought them, and bring on themselves swift destruction. (2 Peter 2:1)*

Perils of False Teaching

> *"Moreover you shall say to them, 'Thus says the Lord: "Will they fall and not rise? Will one turn away and not return? (Jeremiah 8:4)*

> *For fornicators, for sodomites, for kidnappers, for liars, for perjurers, and if there is any other thing that is contrary to sound doctrine, according to the glorious gospel of the blessed God which was committed to my trust (1 Timothy 1:10, 11)*

Some even have their own versions of the bible, differing from the word of God. They have rewritten the word to suit their own doctrines, in order to manipulate others.

> *For the time will come when they will not endure sound doctrine, but according to their own desires, because they have itching ears, they will heap up for themselves teachers; and they will turn their ears away from the truth, and be turned aside to fables. (2 Timothy 4:3, 4)*

Qualities of a Sound Church

> *Holding fast the faithful word as he has been taught, that he may be able, by sound doctrine, both to exhort and convict those who contradict. (Titus 1:9)*

> *But as for you, speak the things which are proper for sound doctrine: (Titus 2:1)*

Jesus is the only way, the truth and the life.

> *Jesus said to him, "I am the way, the truth, and the life. No one comes to the Father except through Me. (John 14:6)*

> *If you love Me, keep My commandments. And I will pray the Father, and He will give you another Helper, that He may abide with you forever— the*

Spirit of truth, whom the world cannot receive, because it neither sees Him nor knows Him; but you know Him, for He dwells with you and will be in you. I will not leave you orphans; I will come to you. (John 14:15-18)

Questions to Consider

1. Who is the leader, pastor or priest?
2. What are their beliefs?
3. What kind of church or congregation do I attend?
4. What doctrine is preached?
5. Is the church filled with the Holy Spirit?
6. Does this church believe the Father, Son, Holy Spirit are One?
7. Does this church disregard opinions that align with scripture?
8. Does the leader focus on compromise and emphasize tolerance?
9. Does the leader focus on Jesus at the Cross or ignore it?
10. Does the leader depress or exhort you each time you leave service?
11. Does the leader value you as a child of the Most High?
12. Does the leader teach directly from the Bible?
13. Does the leader manipulate your intellect as the serpent did?
14. Does the leader serve or simply want to be served?
15. Is this place filled with those unequally yoked and unbelievers?

16. Is this leader a diminisher (*decrease you*) or a multiplier (*increase* you) in the Kingdom of God?

17. Is the church occupied by those that practice adultery, fornication, uncleanness, lewdness, idolatry, sorcery, hatred, contentions, jealousies, outbursts of wrath, selfish ambitions, dissensions, heresies, envy, murderers, drunkenness or revelries? (Galatians 5:18-21)

18. Does this church demonstrate and manifest boldly, love, joy, peace, longsuffering, kindness, goodness, faithfulness, gentleness and self control, which Christ left for us through the work of the Holy Spirit in our lives? (Galatians 5:22-23)

19. Does this church demonstrate and manifest boldly, Spirit, word of wisdom, knowledge, faith, healings, working miracles, prophecy, discerning of spirits, different kinds of tongues and interpretation of tongues, which Christ left for us, through the work of the Holy Spirit? (1Corinthians 12:8-10)

20. Does this church resemble one of the seven churches that the Lord Jesus Christ discussed with John at Patmos?

Watch out, Satan has found his way to the church and his plan is to challenge every good work, which Christ has done on the cross; making many souls to depart from the purpose of God in their lives. What are you hearing, what kind of doctrine have you been listening to? It is time to wake up.

At the dispensation of grace, the garden is not in a location anymore, but is within everyone who accepts Christ, as their Lord and Savior. The Kingdom of God is not by observation, but remains with those who accept Lord Jesus Christ and follow His doctrine all way to the end. Jesus answered them,

> *The Kingdom of God does not come with obser-*
> *vation; nor will they say, See here! Or See there"*
> *For indeed, the kingdom of God is within you.*
> *(Luke 17:20b-21)*

Christ continues to communicate with His children every day, preparing them for His arrival. So, are you listening to Jesus or the old serpent who deceived Eve and forced them out of the garden? Like in the garden, churches are getting deceived by satan, however, the Garden of Eden is now the church. So as a result, many hearts must be cleansed with His precious blood, which Jesus shed for us. Remember, Jesus is coming for His church soon. Are you ready?

> *But the days will come when the bridegroom will*
> *be taken away from them, and then they will fast.*
> *(Matthew 9:15b)*

> *He who has the bride is the bridegroom; but*
> *the friend of the bridegroom; who stands and*
> *hears him, rejoices greatly because of the bride-*
> *groom's voice. Therefore this joy of mine is ful-*
> *filled. (John 3:29)*

> *And said to me Come, I will show you the bride,*
> *the wife of the Lamb. (Revelation 21:9b)*

Now let's look at the church as the spiritual woman or bride of Christ, according to scripture. (Revelation 21:9b) Christ, the bridegroom is coming for His bride, the church.

> *Wives submit to your own husband, as to the Lord. For the husband is head of the wife, as also Christ is the head of the church; and He is the Savior of the body. (Ephesians 5:22-23)*

> *Therefore, just as the church is subject to Christ, so let the wives be to their own husbands in everything. (Ephesians 5:24)*

> *Husbands, love your wives, just as Christ also loved the church and gave Himself for her, that He might sanctify and cleanse her with the washing of water by the word. (Ephesians 5:25-26)*

> *That He might present her to Himself a glorious church, not having spot or wrinkle or any such thing, but that she should be holy and without blemish. (Ephesians 5:27)*

Jesus and John on the Island of Patmos

Jesus Christ addressed some churches in scripture, especially when He visited John on the island of Patmos. His message was very painful because these seven churches that should have known better were found corrupt with things that troubled Him. From the perspective in scripture, in Revelation chapters 1-3, we can conclusively say the appearance of Christ to John on the island of Patmos, was to send a message to these churches, so that they can change from their wicked ways. The message from Jesus to John was to re-affirm churches where the serpent is manifesting himself. They all had unique challenges in their churches.

1. Church in Ephesus: Church had forsaken their first love-Christ.
2. Church in Smyrna: Church under persecution.
3. Church in Pergamum: Church settled in the world.
4. Church in Thyatira: Church in idolatry.
5. Church in Sardis, Church is dead, maintains a believing remnant.
6. Church in Philadelphia: Church in revival.
7. Church Laodicea: Church in its final state of apostasy.

He who overcomes shall be clothed in white garments, and I will not blot his name from the Book of Life: but I will confess his name before My Father and before His angels. (Revelation 3:5)

Take a look at the church, on other hand. Can a church be judged or blamed for the atrocities happening in some of them today? This is why Christ was concerned about these seven churches. He desired from His heart for them to change from their wicked ways and follow the doctrine of the truth He left before departed from this world. Meeting with John at Patmos was to reinforce His warning against the Churches. He reminded them all over again about the price He had paid through the shedding His blood for all sins. God would not send His Son to die again, but to have Him judge all nations, on His second coming. Jesus came to give us life so that we can live our lives more abundantly.

The True Worshiper

We are designed to worship God in Spirit and in truth. As Jesus spoke to the Samaritan woman at the well, He sought to help her do this by imparting God's living water. (John 4:13-14) Jesus sought out this woman personally, to give her abundant life. In the same way, the Father seeks an encounter with each of us that is real and personal. Worship, unfortunately, is often meant to be a bunch of religious rituals, but actually is meant to be an intimate and vital encounter with God. True worship requires full recognition of who God is: holy, sovereign, almighty, loving and merciful. This recognition brings about the realization of our own sinfulness.

True worship is life-changing! It creates within the worshiper's heart a hatred for sin. True worship results in repentance, obedient submission, and a desire for holiness. (Isaiah 6:1-8) True worship generates a desire to show mercy and to express forgiveness. It includes a joyful acceptance of all that God has provided by His grace. True worship is not exclusive. Just as the Samaritan woman rushed off to tell others of her encounter with the Lord, true worship will compel the worshiper to include others, as well. The one who has truly worshiped will have a sense of peace and a confident expectation of what God is about to do. True worship produces a transformed life, reflecting the One who has been worshiped.

But the hour is coming, and now is, when the true worshipers will worship the Father in Spirit and truth; for the Father is seeking such to worship Him. God is Spirit, and those who worship Him must worship in Spirit and Truth. (John 4:23-24)

Jesus Christ, came on the earth to bring mankind back from darkness to the Light, in the Kingdom of heaven, originally lost to satan. Jesus will continue to speak with His church and we must be obedient to His word. Why? His word gives us life. Jesus, the bridegroom, is coming soon for His bride. Are you ready? Who is talking to you, will determine if you are going with Him or not.

CONCLUSION

The legal systems set before Christ couldn't
impeach Him or the woman either.

As mentioned before, knowledge has become the center and core of living on the earth. Yet Christ, is the main tree and the true vine, which we ought to eat from, especially when it comes to knowledge. The knowledge that mankind is seeking today, however, is not from God, but is from this dark world.

Knowledge is a spirit and is a Spirit of the Creator. Those who will eat of it must know His Word. The word of God brings the revelation knowledge of Christ. While the benefit of free will is still in place, think first. The choice(s) we make in our lives ultimately points to either life or death. Remember, the determining factor of our life choices, depends entirely on the source of where one is seeking and gaining knowledge.

Now consider that Satan relentlessly seeks to deceive man whom God has created in His own image. The LORD created us to be general overseers of the planet earth. He gave us dominion over the fish of the sea, and over the fowl of the air, and every living thing that moves upon the earth.

141

(Genesis1:28) Even though, the LORD forewarned Adam and Eve of the consequence of disobedience, Satan managed to seduce and entice the first woman to disregard God's warning and commandment and as a result, Adam and the woman gave their obedience to Satan.

Since his first deception to impeach man and woman in the Garden of Eden, he continues to deceive and accuse the children of God today. Christ came to shed His blood in order to deliver us from the bondages of sin and restore our relationship with our heavenly Father. He was predetermined by His Father to rescue us from condemnation. He is our righteousness and our advocate in heaven.

> *Whom God set forth as a propitiation by His blood, through faith, to demonstrate His righteousness, because in His forbearance God had passed over the sins that were previously committed, to demonstrate at the present time His righteousness, that He might be just and the justifier of the one who has faith in Jesus. (Romans 3:25, 26)*

> *Because He has appointed a day on which He will judge the world in righteousness by the Man whom He has ordained. He has given assurance of this to all by raising Him from the dead." (Acts 17:31)*

> *In this the children of God and the children of the devil are manifest: Whoever does not practice*

righteousness is not of God, nor is he who does not love his brother. (1 John 3:10)

Now I saw heaven opened, and behold, a white horse. And He who sat on him was called Faithful and True, and in righteousness He judges and makes war. (Revelation 19:11)

My little children, these things I write to you, so that you may not sin. And if anyone sins, we have an Advocate with the Father, Jesus Christ the righteous. (1John 2:1)

Jesus Christ stood on behalf of mankind to face every possible accusation from the enemy, the old serpent. Pilate said to them, *"I am innocent of the blood of this just Person. You see to it."* (Matthew 27:24b)

*Now when the tempter came to Him, he said, "If You are the Son of God, command that these stones become bread." But He answered and said, **"It is written, 'Man shall not live by bread alone, but by every word that proceeds from the mouth of God.'"** (Matthew 4:3-4)*

Then the devil took Him up into the holy city, set Him on the pinnacle of the temple, and said to Him, "If You are the Son of God, throw Yourself down. For it is written: 'He shall give His angels charge over you,' and, 'In their hands they shall *bear you up, Lest you dash your foot against a stone.'" **Jesus said to him, "It is written again, 'You shall not tempt the Lord your God.'"*** (Matthew 4:5-7)*

*Again, the devil took Him up on an exceedingly high mountain, and showed Him all the kingdoms of the world and their glory. And he said to Him, "All these things I will give You if You will fall down and worship me." **Then Jesus said to him, "Away with you, Satan! For it is written, 'You shall worship the Lord your God, and Him only you shall serve.'"** (Matthew 4:8-10)*

Then the devil left Him, and behold, angels came and ministered to Him. (Matthew 4:11)

Satan made the first parents focus on themselves rather than God. Any time we shift our focus from God to ourselves, we are listening to a stranger. Satan is looking to impeach those who do not know their position in Christ. So, with Jesus as our advocate, keep these questions in mind, especially while making decisions; but also while considering goals and relationships. From whom are you receiving guidance and direction?

Questions to Consider:

1. What appearances has the serpent manifested lately?
2. What benefit may be motivating your enemy?

3. What benefit may be motivating your decision?
4. What information does the enemy know about you?
5. What information have you volunteered to your enemy?
6. What type of decisions are you in the process of making?
7. What kind of character are you developing?
8. Do you know your character determines your master?
9. Do you know today's decision determine your tomorrow?
10. Who is making suggestions to you?
11. What do you hear God saying to you?
12. What is motivating your decisions?
13. What information are you seeking?
14. Who are you seeking knowledge from?
15. Whose voice are you hearing?

REFERENCE TO PRECIOUS WOMEN OF THE BIBLE

Table 1

DON'T BLAME WOMEN		
She was NOT at the Naming Ceremony		
	Precious Women of the Bible	Summary	Scriptures
1	Eve	Adam's wife, first woman, in conversation with serpent; ate forbidden fruit; tried to hide from God; serpent deceived her; received curse from God; banished with Adam from Eden; Mother of Cain, Abel and Seth.	Gen 2:20-22; 3:1-24, 4:1-4, 25
2	Sarah	Abraham's wife, she gave Hagar to Abram as concubine. Mistreated Hagar so that Hagar ran away, mother of Isaac.	Gen 12:4-20, 17:15-21, 18:10-15, 21:11-7
3	Hagar	Sarah's Egyptian servant and mother of Ishmael; Abraham first son.	Gen 16:1-16; 21:8-21
4	Lot's Wife	Became a pillar of salt when she looked back at Sodom and Gomorrah.	Gen 19:21-26; Luke 17:31-33

5	Lot's Daughter	These daughters, mothered their father's first sons; Moab and Ben-Ammi, the first generation of Moabites and Ammonites.	Gen 19:30-38
6	Rebekah	Isaac's wife, mother of Esau and Jacob, remembered what the LORD told her about her sons. Partnered with God to accomplish the purpose and word of God concerning Jacob.	Gen 24:29-61, 25:19-26, 26:1-11, 27:1-17, 42
7	Rachel	Jacob's second wife, Laban's younger daughter, mother to Joseph and Benjamin, stole Laban gods and died during childbirth of Benjamin.	Gen 29:16-30; 30:22-25, 31:19, 32-35 35:16-25
8	Rahab	Harlot at Jericho helped Joshua's two spies to lodge in and was rewarded. Her father's household was saved. Mother of Boaz.	Josh 2:1-21, 6:17-25, Matt 1:5, Heb 11:31
9	Tamar	Wife of Er, first son of Judah. Tricked Judah into fathering children. Judah slept with her daughter in-law and gave birth to twins, including an ancestor of Jesus.	Gen 38:1-30; Matt 1:3
10	Tamar	Daughter of David, sister of Absalom. Raped by half brother Amnon. Rape avenged by Absalom.	2 Sam. 13:1-33
11	Jochebed	Mother of Moses and Aaron. Hid Moses from the Egyptians. Woman of faith.	Ex 6:19-21, Num 26:25-60 Heb11: 23
12	Pharaoh's Daughter	Found Moses and brought him to the palace, nursed and raised him as her son.	Ex 2:7-10

Table 2

	DON'T BLAME WOMEN		
	She was NOT at the Naming Ceremony		
	Precious Women of the Bible	Summary	Scriptures
13	**Miriam**	Prophetess, sister of Moses and Aaron, spoke against Moses and was covered with Leprosy.	Ex 15:20-21, Num 12:1-15
14	**Deborah**	Prophetess, wife of Lapidoth, Judge in Israel. Fought Sisera's army with Barak.	Gen 35:8, Judges 4:1-16, 5:1-31
15	**Jael**	Wife of Heber. Took Sisera to her tent, pegged him in his temple and killed him. Praised by Deborah.	Judges 4:17-22; 5:5-7, 23-27
16	**Wife of Manoah**	Samson's mother, the Angel of the Lord appeared to her before she conceived her son and told her all about Samson, the kind of child he would be.	Jud 13:2-24
17	**Delilah**	Harlot, Samson revealed the secret of his strength to Delilah the harlot. She cut his hair off.	Jud 16:1-19
18	**Naomi**	Wife of Elimelek, Mother in-law of Ruth, left Bethlehem for Moab during famine and returned as widow with Ruth. Advised Ruth to seek marriage with Boaz. Naomi cared for Ruth's son; Obed.	Ruth 1:1-22, 2: 17, 3:4, 4:13-17
19	**Ruth**	Moabites widow, daughter in-law of Naomi. Went with Naomi' to Jerusalem. Proposed marriage to Boaz. Married Boaz. Gave birth to Obed, an ancestor of David and Jesus.	Ruth 1:3-21, 2:2-17, 3:1-14, 4:1-13, 17-22, Matt 1-5

20	**Hannah**	Wife of Elkanah, Prayed for a Son. Mother of Samuel, dedicated him to the Lord's work.	1Sam 1:1-28, 2:1-21
21	**Michal**	Saul's Daughter, David's wife, Warned David about Saul's plot. Despised in her heart David's victory, was recorded without a child.	1Sam 14:49; 18:17-28; 2 Sam 6:16-23
22	**Anna**	Elderly widow, Witnessed to others about baby Jesus. Prophetess, daughter of Phanuel, from the tribe of Asher.	Luke 2:28, 35-37
23	**Abigail**	Stepsister of David. Married to Jether. Aunt of Joab, David's commander.	2 Sam 17:25, 1Chr. 2:16-17
24	**Abigail**	Wife of Nabal, begged David to spare Nabal's life. Became David's wife. Gave birth to Kileab	1Sam 25:3-42 30:5, 18 3:3

Table 3

DON'T BLAME WOMEN			
She was NOT at the Naming Ceremony			
	Precious Women of the Bible	Summary	Scriptures
25	**Woman or witch of EnDor**	Witch of En Dor, the medium Saul Consulted.	1Sam 28:7-34
26	**Bathsheba**	Uriah's wife, committed adultery with David, became David's wife, conceived and lost first child, mother of Solomon.	2Sam 11:1-3, 12:13-24; 1Kg 1:11-31, 13:25
27	**Rizpah**	Saul's concubine, mother of Mephibosheth who lived in LoDebar.	2Sam 3:7; 21:8-11
28	**Queen of Sheba**	Queen of Sheba, praised Solomon, sought out his Wisdom, brought many gifts to Solomon.	10Kg 1-13, 2Chr 9:1-12
29	**Jezebel**	Wife of King Ahab, worshiped and served Baal, killed prophets of the Lord, killed Naboth, opposed Elijah. Dog eats Jezebel by the wall, symbol of wickedness as Elijah had prophesied.	1Kg 16:31-33; 18:4-19; 19:1-2; 21:1-28, 2Kg 9:30-37; Rev 2:20
30	**Widow of Zarephath**	The Lord sent Prophet Elijah to her house, she was delivered from famine. Her son was revived.	1Kg 17:8-24
31	**Widow Woman**	Wife of a deceased prophet, was able to pay all her debt according to the word of God from Elisha.	2Kg 4:1-7
32	**Shunammite Woman**	Shunammite woman's son was raised from dead by Elisha.	2Kg 4:8-36. 8:1

33	**Huldah**	Huldah the prophetess, wife of Shallum.	2Kg 22:14-20; 2Chr 34:22
34	**Esther**	Became Queen, King Ahaseurus' wife, charged to deliver the Israelites.	Esther 2:1-20
35	**Gomer**	A child of harlotry, wife of Hosea and mother of three sons Jezreel, Lo-Ruhamah and Lo-Ammi.	Hosea 1:1-9, 4-11
36	**Elizabeth**	Mother of John the Baptist.	Luke 1:5-58
37	**Mary**	Mother of Jesus.	Matt 1:16; Luke 1:26-58

Table 4

	Precious Women of the Bible	Summary	Scriptures
	**DON'T BLAME WOMEN**		
	*She was NOT at the Naming Ceremony*		
38	**Woman with flow of blood**	A woman who had an issue of blood for twelve years. Aspired and inspired to touch hem of Jesus garment and got healed.	Matt 9: 18-21, Mark 5:25, Luke 8:43
39	**Herodians, (Herod's Wife)**	Married to king Herod. Motivated and conspired with her seductress dancer daughter against John the Baptist to have his head cut-off. Her daughter demanded John the Baptist's head.	Mark 6:14-28: Matt 14:1-14 Luke 9:7-9
40	**Martha**	Sister of Mary and Lazarus, friend of Jesus.	Luke 10:37-41, Jon 11:1-25-40
41	**Mary**	Mary of Bethany, Sister of Martha and Lazarus, friend of Jesus.	Luke 10:38-41, John 11:1-3
42	**The Syro-Pheonician woman**	Persistent window, cried to Jesus about her daughter who was possessed and the Lord healed her that very hour.	Mark 7:24-30 Matt 15:21-28
43	**Mary Magdalene**	Marry Magdalene was healed of evil spirits and infirmities. Seven demons were cast out of her and she became a follower of Jesus.	Matt 27:55-61, 28:1-3, Mark 15:39-47, 16:1-3 Luke 8:2, 24:10, 19:L25

44	**Salome**	Salome followed Jesus and also bought spices that they might come to anoint Him	Mark 15:39-41; 16:1-3
45	**Dorcas**	Peter raised Tabitah (Dorcas) from death. She was of good works and charitable deeds.	Act 9:35-40
46	**Lydia**	The Lord opened her heart to heed the things spoken by Paul.	Act 16:10-15, 39-40
47	**Abihail**	The second wife of Rehoboam.	1Chr 11:18-19
48	**Abihail**	Wife of Abishur.	2Chr 2:29
49	**Wives of three kings, Jezebel Herodians Wife of Pilate**	**Jezebel,** wife of Ahab, killed prophets of the Lord **Heriodian,** wife of Herod, killed John the Baptist **Wife of Pilate,** encouraged her husband not to do anything to that Man (Jesus).	1Kg 16:31-33, 18:4-19 Mark 6:14-19 Matt 27:15-19
50	**Abishag**	Woman sought after David and he did not know her.	1Kg 1:2-4; 2:13-25

Table 5

DON'T BLAME WOMEN			
She was NOT at the Naming Ceremony			
	Precious Women of the Bible	Summary	Scriptures
51	**Priscilla**	Priscilla wife of Aquila, both travelled with Paul and Invited Paul to live with them.	Act 18:1-3, 17-19, Rom16:3, 1Cor 16:18-20
52	**Dinah**	Daughter of Jacob and Leah, raped by Shechem son of Hamor the Hivite, rape was avenged by her two brothers, Simeon and Levi.	Gen 30:21, 34:1-4, 34:25-29
53	**Abishag**	She was the woman sought for David to care for him but the king did not know her	1Kg 1:2-22
54	**Woman of Tekoa**	Joab used this woman to communicate with the king.	2 Sam 14:1-18
55	**Woman of Proverbs with Seductive and flattering words**	Seductive and flattering words.	Prov 2:6
56	**Woman of Proverbs with mouth smoother than oil**	Mouth smoother than oil.	Pro 5:5-11
57	**Woman in the basket**	Woman sitting inside the basket and other two women were flying between the earth and heaven.	Zech 5:5-11

58	**Woman costly fragrant**	Brought an alabaster flask of fragrant oil to anoint Him.	Matt 26:6-8, Luke 7:36-38, 45-47
59	**Woman caught in adultery**	This woman was caught in adultery, and was brought to Jesus. Jesus replied to the accusers.	Jon 8:1-5
60	**Women at Solomon's court**	Solomon Judged among his people. Two prostitute women came before King Solomon about the death of one of their sons.	1Kg 3:16-28
61	**Abital**	Wife of David.	1Sam 3:4; 1Chr 3:3
62	**Adah**	Wife of Lamech.	Gen 4:19-23
63	**Wife of Pilate**	Wife of Pilate encouraged her husband the Pilate, have nothing to do with Jesus, about his death.	Matt 27:17-19

More Exciting Titles
by MATTHEW DARE O'DUNLAMI

Jesus in the House Ministries

P.O. Box 567

Sicklerville, NJ 08081, USA

Website: www.JesusintheHouse.org

Email: JesusinHouseMinistries@gmail.com

Available at www.JesusintheHouse.org
Also at Xulon Press and
Bookstores Worldwide

HOLY SPIRIT MANUFACTURED PRAYER

As we are fast approaching His next coming, I believe the LORD wants to reveal His plan, His place, His provision, and His purpose for our lives. But for us to get there, we must partner with Him through vigorous prayer. Do not just pray, but pray with understanding. How we pray can determine the urgency at which our prayers are answered. I am sure victory is waiting for you. Prayer Reveals the Mind of God; Prayer Helps to Renew Our Mind-Set; Prayer Shows Humility to Our Creator; Prayer Keeps Us Spiritually Alert for Kingdom Purposes; Prayer Prepares us for the Second Coming of Our Lord Jesus.

ISBN 9781591609247 – Soft Copy
ISBN 9781619043572 – Hard Copy
Available at your local Christian bookstore

THE PROPHETIC ORDINANCE BLESSING

The Prophetic Ordinance Blessing contains over 2,000 consecrated prophetic blessings of God that you can release through utterances and pronouncements over yourself, your spouse, your children and your entire generation. I encourage you to use this powerful Devotional and see what God will do for you and your loved ones victoriously. Prayer! It's the prophetic ordinance blessing.

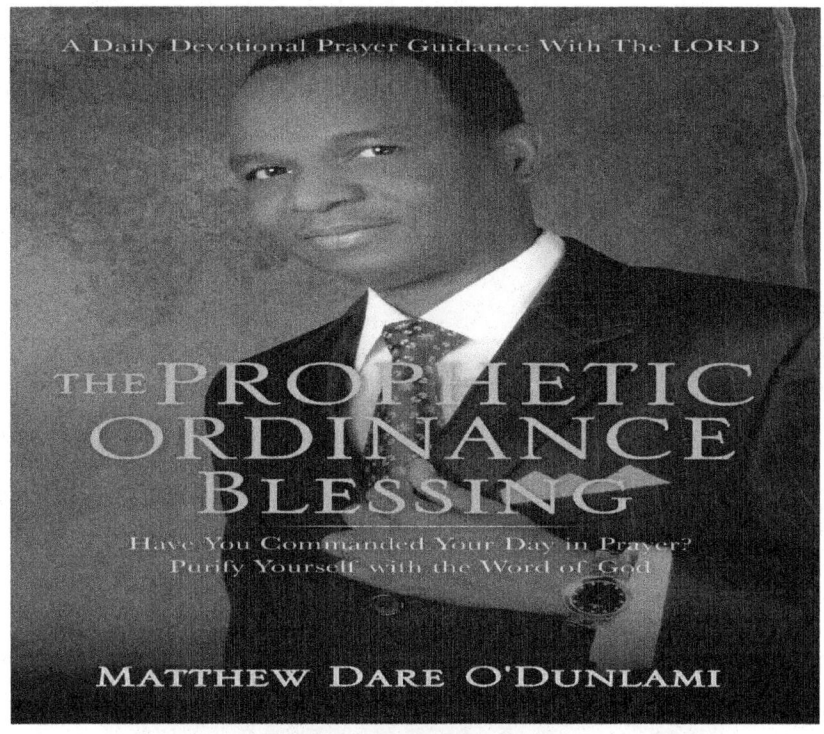

ISBN 9781628716160
Available at your local Christian bookstore

GEBET VOM
HEILIGEN GEIST PRODUZIERT
(Holy Spirit Manufactured Prayer in German Translation)

Während wir uns schnell Seinem nächsten Kommen nähern, glaube ich, dass der HERR Seinen Plan, Seinen Ort, Seine Versorgung, und Seine Absicht für unsere Leben offenbaren will. Aber damit wir dort hin kommen, müssen wir mit Ihm durch energisches Gebet als Partner kooperieren. Beten Sie nicht einfach nur so, sondern beten Sie mit Verständnis. Wie wir beten, kann die Dringlichkeit bestimmen, mit der unsere Gebete erhört werden. Ich bin sicher, dass Sieg auf Sie wartet. Gebet Offenbart die Gedanken Gottes; Gebet Hilft Unsere Geisteshaltung zu Erneuern; Gebet Zeigt Unserem Schöpfer Demut; Gebet Lässt Uns Geistlich Alarmiert bleiben für die Absichten des Königreiches; Gebet Bereitet Uns für das Zweite Kommen Unseres Herrn Jesus vor.

ISBN 9781628714302
Available at your local Christian Bookstore

FIRSTBORN SYNDROME

Firstborn Syndrome will reveal, the secret behind the mysterious antediluvian firstborn syndrome that has paralyzed human race since the Creations. Enemy violently waging war against humanity and everything the LORD created or made first. ***Understanding your ancestry can momentously change your generations***. First thing created, physically and spiritually will require the Second to be perfected, why? Firstborn Syndrome will engage and reposition you to know your worth in Christ Jesus and to enjoy the full inheritance through **His Divine Exchange Power** that He has bought for you. It is about your original purpose in life, and about the existence of a divine that purpose, behind your creation the meaning of your life through His Blood.

FIRSTBORN SYNDROME

Antediluvian Syndrome Annulled By the Blood of Jesus Christ

MATTHEW DARE O'DUNLAMI

Understanding Our Ancestry Can Momentously Transform our Lives and Generations

ISBN
Available at your local Christian bookstore

Jesus Christ Name Guarantee Victorious lifestyles

Jesus Christ Name Guarantee Everlasting Life

Jesus Christ Name Insulate, Incubate and Consecrate

Jesus Christ Name Guarantee Blissful and Blessed life

Jesus Christ Name Blotted-out the Handwriting of Enemy

Jesus Christ Name Counter the Attempt and Device of Satan

Jesus Christ Name Destroyed All Evil Interrogations

JESUS IN THE HOUSE MINISTRIES INC

P.O. Box 567
Sicklerville, NJ 08081, USA

Website: www.JesusintheHouse.org
Email: JesusinHouseMinistries@gmail.com

Additional copies of this book and other
book titles from Jesus in the House Ministries Inc. are
available at our website, Xulon Press and your local
bookstores

CPSIA information can be obtained at www.ICGtesting.com
Printed in the USA
BVOW08s1344090315

390611BV00006B/10/P

9 781629 522289